FREUD'S ODYSSEY

FREUD'S ODYSSEY

Psychoanalysis and the End of Metaphysics

STAN DRAENOS

Yale University Press
New Haven and London

Published with assistance from the
Louis Stern Memorial Fund.

Designed by Sally Harris
and set in Caledonia type.
Printed in the United States of America by
The Alpine Press, Stoughton, Mass.

Library of Congress Cataloging in Publication Data

Draenos, Stan, 1945–
  Freud's odyssey.
  Bibliography: p.
  Includes index.
  1. Psychoanalysis.   2. Freud, Sigmund, 1856–
1939.   I. Title.
BF173.F85D66   150.19′52   82-1961
    ISBN 0-300-02791-5   AACR2

10 9 8 7 6 5 4 3 2 1

Contents

Acknowledgments

Special thanks are due to Paul Antze, James Miller, and Robert M. Tostevin for helping me at critical junctures to see what needed to be seen. Thanks are also due to Alkis Kontos and Christian Lenhardt for their unfailing solidarity and support. I am grateful to the *Canadian Journal of Political and Social Theory*, where some of the ideas in this book first appeared. Finally, thanks to my wife, Sylvia Diveky, who always spoke her mind.

Introduction

Until recently, interpreters of Freud's thought consistently placed it in the context of philosophy and social theory. Differences aside, the interpretations of Philip Rieff, Herbert Marcuse, Jürgen Habermas, and Paul Ricoeur engaged Freud on a common, if contested, terrain. Marx, Dilthey, Nietzsche, and behind them, Descartes, Kant, and Hegel, defined the constellation of thought to which psychoanalysis belonged. Freud's relation to the mainstream of continental philosophy seemed at once undeniable and essential to understanding psychoanalysis at all. Then, when at least that much seemed settled, the centrality of the biological and positivistic dimension of Freud's writings was rediscovered, transposing the locus of his achievement into the domain of the natural sciences. In securing a place for psychoanalysis in the history of science, Frank Sulloway's *Freud, Biologist of the Mind* cast an odd and disorienting light on the interpretations that saw Freud in the context of philosophy and social theory.

This study does not seek to adjudicate this fundamental conflict of interpretations—to decide between the vision of Freud, the natural scientist, and Freud, the social philosopher. Its effect, however, is to show why Freud's writings have engendered both readings, and why both are misleading. My contention is that the psychoanalytic venture was conceived as a response to the decisive victory natural science won over philosophy through Darwin. This study illuminates the path Freud marked out between the tradition of reflective philosophy and the discoveries of evolutionary biology. My claim is that the exploration of psychoanalytic theory

1

within these terms of reference affords a fresh insight into the tensions, the transformations, and above all, the relentless dynamic of Freud's thought.

Freud's way between reflective philosophy and evolutionary biology signifies no intellectual synthesis, no fusion of disparate influences or modes of thought. Rather, it signifies Freud's recognition of the unprecedented situation of understanding it was his fate to inherit and the boldness with which he seized that fate and sought to master it. For Freud, as for Nietzsche, that situation was defined by the eclipse of the transcendent, the death of metaphysics. Freud's self-proclaimed hostility toward German metaphysics was also a denial of his own earliest impulses. Psychoanalysis was an attempt to satisfy those impulses by canalizing them within the sober cognitions of science.

My central concern is to show how Freud was possessed by deeply held but contradictory intellectual commitments, how psychoanalytic theory was a bold attempt to reconcile those contradictions without simply bypassing them, and how the development of psychoanalytic thought was propelled by the tensions those contradictions produced. The inherent interest I found in following this intellectual odyssey is that Freud's commitments are not exclusive to him. Rather, they are representative of tenets and assumptions which have been shared by that literate public whose understanding is rooted in the Enlightenment. In the development of Freud's thought I saw those tenets and assumptions crystallize and then dissolve in a way I felt to be particularly illuminating. I do not, however, try to claim for Freud a monopoly on insight or to turn him into some kind of Hegelian *Weltgeist*. My effort has been to see if I could discover the hidden theoretical motives of a major architect of the modern outlook.

The story I attempt to tell, then, is that of a thinker who was possessed of a conflicted theoretical will—a man whose passion for truth and for the solace of truth was displaced from its original aim by the triumph of the natural sciences. The odyssey of Freud's thought consists in his relentless striving to return, via the circuitous route of natural science, to his spiritual place of origin—philosophy. The story unfolds in three parts. Part I is concerned with metapsychology (a term Freud coined in the 1890s) and the foundations of the psychoanalytic perspective. Of necessity, it begins obliquely in chapter 1 with a discussion of a fundamental contradiction that pervades Freud's writings. My effort is to lead the reader to the metapsychological dimension that that contradiction bears witness to. Chapter 2 identifies and elucidates that dimension in terms of Freud's relation to Darwinism and Cartesian dualism. Chapters 3 and 4 explain how *The Interpretation of Dreams* and the *Three Essays on the Theory of Sexuality* mark a decisive leap beyond Freud's earlier formulations and lay the foundations of psychoanalytic theory in accordance with the requirements of metapsychology.

In part II, the issues raised in part I are placed within the broader situation of understanding to which psychoanalytic theory is a response. The three chapters of "Psychoanalysis, Evolution, and the End of Metaphysics" clarify Freud's way between reflective philosophy and evolutionary biology and show how that way informs the psychoanalytic understanding of life.

Part III is concerned with the metamorphosis that psychoanalytic theory undergoes after *Totem and Taboo*. The odysseylike nature of Freud's quest becomes manifest when the problem of cultural meaning forces him to overcome the limitations of his original theoretical framework in order to remain faithful to his original insights and to fulfill his original aims. The focus is on the theory of the instincts and its problems, where the covert philosophical animus of the psychoanalytic venture finally breaks through to the surface of Freud's thought.

The analysis of Freud's writings pursued in these pages falls somewhere between philosophy and intellectual biography. It is the biography of Freud's theoretical daimon. My interest in this particular kind of enterprise can be traced back to the American studies seminars I attended at Berkeley in the 1960s and to my teacher Michael Rogin. Fundamentally, however, Freud's writings themselves, and the need to understand they created in me, were decisive in determining the nature of the analysis. A method is followed here only in the sense proposed by Aristotle—in the sense, that is, that the subject matter itself suggests the appropriate way to be followed. As I was completing the original draft in the summer of 1978, a metaphorical expression of what I was doing occurred to me and has stuck ever since. The act of interpretation, it seemed to me, is like the act of sculpting, which Michelangelo once described as freeing the form that lies hidden within the block of granite. Like the block of granite, the thinker's text impresses itself upon the interpreter with a force that weighs upon him and moves him. Interpretation is the interpreter's act of resistance to the text's inertial force. In working against its density, the interpreter at once releases from the text a hidden form and frees himself of his burden.

PART I

THE FOUNDATIONS OF
THE PSYCHOANALYTIC
PERSPECTIVE

The disregarding of conscious conditions
and the acceptance of the metapsychological
way of thought are as difficult
as they are indispensable.

—Freud to Lou Andreas-Salomé, 1915

CHAPTER 1

The Metapsychological Threshold

A contradiction runs through Freud's writings like a fault line. It arises from the fact that psychoanalysis presents itself as knowledge of two different kinds. On the one hand, psychoanalysis takes the form of an understanding of mind obtained through the disclosure of hidden meaning in dreams and neurotic symptoms. On the other, psychoanalysis takes the form of an explanation of mind secured in the elucidation of the mechanisms and systemic relations of a "mental apparatus."

To bring these two forms of knowledge together within one science is like trying to square a circle. For they carry with them visions of mind that are fundamentally at odds. In seeking to understand mind through the interpretation of meaning, Freud treats the mental as the property of a subject and his inner life. In seeking to explain mind as mechanism, he places mental phenomena among the natural objects of the external world. Mind as meaning and mind as mechanism, however, lie on opposing sides of the great divide first enunciated in Descartes's famous dualism, in the distinction between the *res cogitans* and the *res extensa,* consciousness and matter, subject and object.

Freud was by no means blind to the force of this dualism. On the contrary, he acknowledged it explicitly. The "antithesis" between the inner and the outer, subject and object, he wrote in 1915, "remains, above all, sovereign in our intellectual activity and creates for research the basic situation which no efforts can alter."[1] Yet nothing is more characteristic of his writings than the attempt to define an idiom straddling both sides of the dualism. The crucial psychoanalytic concept of "displacement," for instance, is drawn from hydraulics but is deployed to specify one of the factors governing meaning distortion in dreams and neuroses. What to Freud's mind necessitated the development of this peculiar idiom, and what justified the epistemological hazards he thus ran, was his conviction that psychoanalytic science was focused upon a unique entity—the unconscious. "No doubt the Ucs. [unconscious] is the right mediator between the physical and the mental," he wrote Groddeck in 1917, "perhaps it is the long-sought-for 'missing link.' "[2]

The contradiction that runs through psychoanalytic discourse is thus not the result of an oversight or epistemological blunder on Freud's part. Rather, it points to something essential in the venture he undertook. "Fundamental and flagrant contradictions rarely occur in second-rate writers, in whom they can be discounted," Hannah Arendt once observed. "In the work of great authors they lead into the very center of their work and are the most important clue to a true understanding of their problems and new insights."[3] With regard to Freud, Arendt's observation is exact. The contradiction in Freud's thought is the passageway into its covert theoretical problems and novel insights. By examining more closely the nature of the contradiction, we shall make our way to the threshold across which those problems and insights rise to view.

In the *Introductory Lectures* (1915–16) Freud raises the question what kind of science psychoanalysis is by contrasting it with chemistry, physiology, and anatomy. His audience is composed of medical students.

> In medical training you are accustomed to *see* things. You see an anatomical preparation, the precipitate of a chemical reaction, the shortening of a muscle as a result of the stimulation of its nerves. Later on, patients are demonstrated before your senses. . . . In the surgical departments you are witnesses of the active measures taken to bring help to patients. . . . Even in psychiatry the demonstration of patients with their altered facial expressions, their mode of speech and their behaviour, affords you plenty of observations which leave a deep impression on you. Thus . . . you gain a direct contact with the objects exhibited and feel yourselves convinced of the existence of the new facts through your own perception.

In psychoanalysis, we learn, "everything is different. Nothing takes place in a psycho-analytic treatment but an interchange of words between the patient and the analyst."[4] To complicate matters further, the psychoanalytic interchange of words cannot be publicly demonstrated. The presence of an outside observer effectively brings the analytic dialogue to an end.

In drawing this contrast between psychoanalysis and the sciences traditionally associated with medicine, Freud wishes to indicate something more fundamental than just the pedagogical difficulties his subject confronts him with. He wishes to point out a difference in the observational basis that distinguishes psychoanalysis from the other medical sciences. Physiology and anatomy are unequivocally empirical sciences of natural phenomena, with all the scientific respectability attached thereto. They rely upon the senses both as the means through which the phenomena to be explained are grasped and as the ultimate referent of the concepts through which their explanation is achieved.

Freud is frank about the absence of this kind of empirical basis for psychoanalysis. In psychoanalysis, an interchange of words provides the field of observation within which phenomena are grasped and to which explanatory concepts are ultimately referred. This observational field does not consist of "visible and tangible" things that appear to the senses. Instead, it is sustained wholly in the sphere of significations opened up by the dialogic interchange. In the same passages from the *Introductory Lectures,* Freud describes this dialogue more fully.

> The patient talks, tells of his past experiences and present impressions, complains, confesses to his wishes and emotional impulses. The doctor listens, tries to direct the patient's processes of thought, exhorts, forces his attention in certain directions, gives him explanations and observes the reactions of understanding or rejection which he in this way provokes in him.[5]

The struggle of wills that characterizes the analytic dialogue exists for a reason. The sphere of significations opened up by the psychoanalytic process is generated in the effort to overcome the patient's resistances—resistances that are the sure signs that ideas have been repressed into the unconscious. "The whole theory of psycho-analysis," we are told in the *New Introductory Lectures,* "is . . . built up on the *perception of the resistances* offered to us by the patient when we attempt to make his unconscious conscious to him" (my italics).[6]

The dynamics of the analytic dialogue suggest a physical process of forces in opposition—and, indeed, the "dynamic standpoint" is one of the fundamental "metapsychological" levels upon which psychoanalytic theory is based. But the dynamic standpoint does not capture the essence of the dialogue. The struggle of wills centers on the discovery of hidden meaning—meaning which the patient not only conceals from the world but, "as a homogeneous personality, he will not admit to himself."[7] Psychoanalysis entails the discovery and recovery by the subject of parts of his self that have split off and become alien to him. These split off, repressed contents have entered his unconscious, which expresses itself symbolically and cryptically in neurotic symptoms, dreams, and parapraxes. Neurosis is the manifestation of repressed ideas that have returned by devious pathways not under the control of the ego to distort and disrupt the continuity of the subject's personality. The dream is a neurotic symptom permissible even within a normal psychical economy, since the repressed wishes it expresses are harmless. The subject is protected by the "motor paralysis" of sleep from carrying them out. In the neurotic, however, the repressed contents have returned to haunt his waking life in the form of incomprehensible compulsions, fears, and hysterias. The dissociated ego becomes a self-clarified whole through the process of deciphering these unintelligible expressive manifestations and making them part of the transparent system of meaning that constitutes the subject's self-understanding.

This is the work of the psychoanalytic dialogue. If the appeal to facticity of the sciences associated with medical training is based on what appears to the senses, the appeal of psychoanalysis is to the "sense" that appears to the understanding in the course of the psychoanalytic interpretation of meaning. Freud himself uses the word *Sinn* in this second way as he demonstrates in the *Introductory Lectures* the existence of unconscious motives and intentions—and finally of "the unconscious" itself—through the interpretation of dreams and parapraxes. It is as if he were trying to tell us, through the suggestive dual signification the word *Sinn* bears, that psychoanalysis, too, is rooted in the senses and is thereby a fully legitimate empirical science on a par with the physical sciences. But he is also quick to clarify that by sense he means nothing more than "the intention [that a psychical process] serves and its position in a psychical continuity. In most of our researches we can replace 'sense' by 'intention' or 'purpose.' "[8] Thus the dual signification of the word sense serves in fact to dramatize the distinction between those empirical sciences whose phenomena are provided by the visible and tangible and psychoanalysis, a science of interpretation that relies upon "finding a hidden sense in something."[9] Psychoanalysis has its field of observation in the sphere of significations opened up in the dynamics of the psychoanalytic dialogue.

The separation of psychoanalysis from the other sciences on the basis of the kind of phenomena it deals with is definitive in Freud's writings. He often repeated and, with the important exception of *Beyond the Pleasure Principle,* never violated the admonition that "psycho-analysis must keep itself free from any hypothesis that is alien to it, whether of an anatomical, chemical or physiological kind, and must operate entirely with purely psychological auxiliary ideas."[10] The positive side of this stricture is the epistemological assertion that "all our knowledge is invariably bound up with consciousness. We can come to know even the *Ucs.* [unconscious] only by making it conscious."[11] The reason for confining psychoanalysis to psychological phenomena and concepts it that

> it is easy to describe the unconscious and follow its developments if it is approached from the direction of its relation to consciousness, with which it has so much in common. On the other hand, there still seems no possibility of approaching it from the direction of physical events.[12]

Thus, when he says that "our acts of consciousness . . . are immediate data and cannot be further explained by any sort of description," and that the "fact of consciousness" is "without parallel" and "defies all explanation or description,"[13] his purpose, obviously, is not to argue against the possibility of discovering psychological explanations for conscious processes, but, instead, to defend those "immediate data" against physicalistic efforts to explain them away as mere epiphenomena—as gratuitous side effects of material processes.

Freud's careful utterances seem to throw into doubt our earlier assertion that psychoanalytic discourse advances contradictory ways of knowing mind. In terms of its field of phenomena, at least, psychoanalysis stands clearly and unequivocally in the domain of the *res cogitans.* Freud's contradiction reappears, however, in the simple fact that he regarded psychoanalysis as a *natural* science—an investigation of the "mental apparatus" that, having developed "in the attempt to explore the external world," is also "a constituent part of that world."[14] Freud always thought of the mind, in Raymond Fancher's apt phrase, as an "energy-processing organ."[15] Freud's metapsychological description of its functioning was articulated in mechanistic-energic concepts that were the universal concepts of Enlightenment science.

To be sure, Freud was careful in this metapsychological description not to violate the stricture against the importation of foreign hypotheses into the explanation of psychological phenomena. The mechanistic-energic description Freud deployed was developed with a view to fitting it to psychological phenomena. The description represents psychological phenomena in the language of the material reality that presumably underlies them. Thus, in his *Autobiographical Study* Freud characterizes metapsychology as "a method of approach according to which every mental process is considered in relation to three co-ordinates, which I described as *dynamic, topographical* and *economic,* respectively; . . . this seemed to me to represent the furthest goal that psychology could attain."[16] The *dynamics* of the mind refers to an interplay of forces, a calculus of energies in opposition, distributed *topographically* in space and governed by an *economics,* whose tendency is to keep the total quantities of energy in the mental apparatus constant or as low as possible.

The metapsychological description does not reduce mental phenomena to physical phenomena, however. Instead, each of the three coordinates of Freud's metapsychology formalizes psychical phenomena within natural scientific terms of reference. By deploying this coordinate system in a kind of method of triangulation, Freud hoped to locate mental processes on the ontological map projected by the natural sciences for the data of external reality—for phenomena, that is, that arise independently of consciousness. In this crucial sense, psychoanalysis rejects the identification of mind with the domain of the *res cogitans.* For psychoanalysis, mind is a product of nature like the other entities of the external world. Thus,

> the hypothesis we have adopted of a physical apparatus extended in space, expediently put together, developed by the exigencies of life, which gives rise to the phenomena of consciousness only at one particular point and under certain conditions—this hypothesis has put us in a position to establish psychology on foundations similar to those of any other science, such, for instance, as physics.[17]

Freud's metapsychology, then, seeks to describe the mind as a natural object while remaining faithful to the essentially subjective nature of psychological phenomena. The attempt simply does not wash. Freud's metapsychology does affect the status of his phenomenal domain. In relating mental processes to dynamic, topographical, and economic coordinates, Freud is no longer dealing with the generation of meaning but with the processing of energy. The derivation of a physicalist model of the mind from an observational field whose phenomena appear in the dialogic struggle to discover and recover lost meaning creates a serious epistemological rift in the theoretical fabric of psychoanalytic thought. Can the contradiction between these two levels of discourse—between the physicalistic description of the mind as a natural object and the hermeneutic practice of psychoanalysis as the discovery and recovery of lost meaning—be resolved? In other words, can Freud's psychology be reconciled with his metapsychology?

In *Knowledge and Human Interests* Jürgen Habermas attributes the epistemological rift of Freudian theory to the "scientistic self-misunderstanding of metapsychology." "Because Freud was caught up from the beginning in a scientistic self-understanding, he succumbed to an objectivism that regresses immediately from the level of self-reflection to contemporary positivism."[18] Metapsychology understands itself as giving a scientific basis to psychoanalysis, while all it really manages to do is correlate "mentalistic expressions (such as impulse, stimulation, pain, pleasure, wish) and physical processes (such as energy quanta, energy tension and discharge, and, as a system property, the tendency toward efflux of energy)."[19] The clear implication of Habermas's point is that the language of Freud's metapsychology is, in essence, analogical. Thus, "the energy-distribution model only creates the semblance that psychoanalytic statements are about measurable transformations of energy."[20]

Habermas's critique does not seek to challenge the validity of psychoanalysis as such. Instead, it seeks to salvage the validity of psychoanalytic insight from the untenable scientism that encumbers it. Since "Freud unswervingly retained the analytic dialogue as the sole empirical basis not only for the development of metapsychology but for the validity of psychoanalytic theory as well," the critique of Freudian metapsychology need not affect the "real status of the science."[21] That real status lies in the theory of self-reflection that psychoanalysis embodies. "The *act of understanding* to which [psychoanalysis] leads is self-reflection."[22] Seen in this light, psychoanalysis stands on its own without need of Freud's ill-conceived metapsychology.[23]

Habermas's reading of Freud is surgical in precision and cogency. Through an immanent critique, only partially sketched here, its purpose is to demonstrate psychoanalysis to be a form of self-reflection bound up with the interests of life activity. Psychoanalysis provides an example of the reflective self-constitution of knowledge that, as self-knowledge, is no longer contemplative, but is instead an emancipatory practice. So understood, psychoanalysis serves purposes internal to the argument of *Knowledge and Human Interests*, which need not concern us here.

What does concern us is that Habermas's reading of Freud obviates consideration of the theoretical motives that prompted Freud to coin the term *metapsychology* and pursue the venture in the first place. Habermas's critique is correct. The epistemological disjunction between the interpretation of meaning and the processing of energy exists. But on this matter Paul Ricoeur's *Freud and Philosophy*, which is also concerned with reading psychoanalysis as a reflective enterprise, makes, I think, the essential point. Like Habermas, Ricoeur must come to terms with the "mixed discourse" of psychoanalysis, which "at times states conflicts of forces subject to an energetics, at times relations of meaning subject to a hermeneutics."[24] In the face of the disjunction between "explanation in terms of energy" and "understanding in terms of phenomenology," however, Ricoeur observes frankly: "Freudianism exists only on the basis of its refusal of that disjunction."[25] This refusal is crucial to an understanding of the psychoanalytic odyssey.

Habermas does not consider the provocative fact that Freud's first determinate use of the term *metapsychology*, in a letter to Wilhelm Fleiss of March 10, 1898, associates it not with the coordinate system we have described above, but with biology.[26] Though this use of the term never appears in his published writings, it nonetheless provides an essential clue, as we shall see, to the significance of "biology" in Freud's thought. Freud later assigns to this biologistic element the title "the theory of the instincts," which in 1924 he calls "the most important but at the same time the least complete portion of psychoanalytic theory."[27] In the theory of the instincts Freud must make good the refusal of the disjunction Ricoeur refers to. Habermas, on the other hand, obviates the issues at stake in Freud's instinct theory through a reformulation that roots it unequivocally in the "meaning structures of the life-world." The Freudian instincts, he tells us, are in fact "twisted and diverted intentions that have turned from conscious motives into causes and subjected communicative action to the causality of 'natural' conditions. This is the causality of fate, and not of nature, because it prevails through the symbolic means of the mind."[28]

The rooting of instinct theory in the meaning structures of the life world may have its justification as a reconstruction of Freud's thought that turns it into a theory of reflection. But to do so closes us off from the metapsychological insight that instinct theory was intended to express. For another way of stating the meaning of metapsychology is that it signifies a dimension of human reality which can never be captured in the movement of reflection. That is why the experiences arising out of the biological function of sexuality turn out to be perfectly suited as the guiding thread for the specifically psychoanalytic form of reflection.

The internal contradiction of psychoanalytic theory has thus led us to the threshold of what I hope to demonstrate are its most interesting problems. In order to enter and gain our bearings within this largely uncharted territory, we must begin our consideration of Freud again. This time, we shall attempt to reconstruct the immanent movement of his thought in a way that makes explicit the unarticulated questions that provoked it and the primordial insight that sustained its speculative vitality. That is, we shall attempt to disclose the foundations of the psychoanalytic perspective.

CHAPTER 2

The Origins of the
Psychoanalytic Perspective

The Darwinian Setting

Evolutionary speculation was widespread in Europe for some time
before Darwin's voyage of discovery. Nonetheless, Darwin's success in establishing a mechanical explanation for the origin and development of life phenomena was a landmark in the life history of
Western understanding. The realm of organic being, which had so
long eluded the snare of a science of efficient causality, was finally
captured within its explanatory net. "The scientific revolution," as
John Dewey put it, "found its climax in the *Origin of Species*."[1]

The tacit yet pervasive background of psychoanalytic theory is
Darwin's comprehension of vital existence within the mechanistic
discipline of natural science. Writing in *An Autobiographical
Study* about his choice of a medical career, Freud recalls, "the theories of Darwin, which were then [1873] of topical interest, strongly
attracted me, for they held out hope of an extraordinary advance in
our understanding of the world."[2] And when Freud came to reflect
upon the "three blows to human self-love" dealt to mankind by the
researches of science, Darwin's intellectual triumph was chosen as
the second in a sequence beginning with the Copernican revolution
and culminating in psychoanalysis itself. Freud's discussion of evolution here concerns not the significance of Darwin's theory for scientific knowledge but its significance for human self-understanding.
His description of that impact also articulates the understanding that
forms the point of departure for psychoanalytic theory.

> In the course of the development of civilization, man acquired a dom-
> inating position over his fellow-creatures in the animal kingdom. Not
> content with this supremacy, however, he began to place a gulf be-

tween his nature and theirs. He denied the possession of reason to them, and to himself he attributed an immortal soul, and made claims to a divine descent which permitted him to break the bond of community between him and the animal kingdom. . . .

We all know that little more than half a century ago the researches of Charles Darwin and his collaborators and forerunners put an end to this presumption on the part of man. Man is not a being different from animals or superior to them; he himself is of animal descent, being more closely related to some species and more distantly to others. The acquisitions he has subsequently made have not succeeded in effacing the evidences, both in his physical structure and in his mental dispositions of his parity with them.[3]

That Darwin had restored the "bond of community" between man and his fellow creatures was, indeed, a necessary consequence of the theory of evolution argued in the *Origin of Species* (1859). When Freud sought to elaborate psychoanalysis as a natural science, he was simply adhering to what, for the educated man living in the wake of Darwin, was a necessary truth. Psychoanalysis was a natural science because the mind is a natural object. The mind is a natural object because, by the logic of evolution, men are natural beings who share with their animal brethren a common history of descent. For evolutionary science the mental powers that, among other things, distinguish *homo sapiens* from the animal species have by logical necessity evolved from lower and simpler properties of vital existence. After Darwin the continuity between mental and organic properties, however it might be construed, was a matter of course. Thus Darwin could assert with confidence, but without yet having tried his hand at explaining the phenomenon of man, "In the future I see open fields for far more important researches. Psychology will be based on a new foundation, that of the necessary acquirement of each mental power and capacity by gradation. Light will be thrown on the origin of man and his history."[4]

Freud's psychoanalytic theory does not carry out the program of a Darwinian psychology. Far from it. Darwin's own way of construing the continuity of mental and organic properties was already laid out in the *Origin of Species*, and it bore little resemblance to what was to be Freud's endeavor. The essentials of a Darwinian psychology— and it is a psychology, we should note, that embraces plants and cuckoos as well as humans—are found in the mechanistic explanation of patterned behavior, that is, of instinct in the ethological sense. The fundamental mechanism in the evolution of organic form, Darwin discovered, is the interplay of variation and natural selection. The offspring of any species manifest slight variations of form, some of which improve the relative chances for the survival and reproduction of the organisms possessing them. Working by elimination under the pressure of changing organic and inorganic conditions of life, natural selection preserves and accumulates favorable variations, resulting, through immense stretches of time, in the branching of life into a multiplicity of species, each branch defining a species history—a phylogenetic sequence of form changes of which every living species member is only the latest outcome. It thus became conceivable that from the spontaneous emergence of the simplest life forms out of the primeval soup, the whole kingdom of life, with its infinite variety and complexity, could have evolved.

The essence of Darwinian psychology consists in identifying inherited instinctual behavior patterns or potentials and fitting them into this mechanistic scheme. "It will be admitted," Darwin tells us, "that instincts are as important as corporeal structure for the welfare of each species." And if even slight variations in the instincts can be demonstrated, he sees "no difficulty in natural selection preserving and continually accumulating variations of instinct to any extent that may be profitable." Thus the production of each complex instinct may be attributed to "the effects of the natural selection of what may be called accidental variations of instincts;—that is, of variations produced by the same unknown causes which produce the slight deviations of bodily structure." We can feel certain, then, that the "canon of *'Natura non facit saltum'* [nature does not make a leap] applies with almost equal force to the instincts as to bodily organs."[5]

The projected psychology springing from a Darwinian treatment of instinct—which when applied to man would constitute an essential part of evolutionary anthropology—is fundamentally behavioral. Its observational field consists in the identification of externally observed patterns in the activity of organisms with a view to interpreting them in terms of their utility for preserving the life of the organism or of the species to which it belongs. Psychoanalysis, on the other hand, is distinguished by its exclusive concern with human psychology, but more essentially, by a fundamental epistemological decision to confine itself wholly to the phenomena of consciousness for its evidences. And, in this latter sense, psychoanalysis clearly does not carry out the program of an evolutionary psychology for the species *homo sapiens.* What, then, is the relationship I propose to demonstrate between Darwin's theory of evolution and Freud's psychoanalysis?

Evolutionary science is concerned with explaining the origins and development of living nature. The nature it brings into the view of natural science turns out to be a "nature with man in it," as J. H. Randall has put it.[6] The mental powers and capacities that humans exhibit more emphatically than other organic beings thus present science with the problem of accounting for mind. It takes that problem as one whose terms of reference are already defined by the mechanics of natural selection. Insofar as evolutionary science concerns itself with the human mind, it seeks to fit the mental evidences *homo sapiens* manifests within the framework of those mechanics. It does this by identifying "mind" with externally observed patterns of behavior and asking what survival advantages accrue to *homo sapiens* from them. Evolutionary psychology would in this way extend the explanatory reach of the evolutionary causal scheme to embrace body and soul the phenomenon of man.[7]

The provenance of Freud's psychoanalysis is wholly different. Freud's thinking unfolds in the shadow of man's discovery that he is an animal, but not as an extension of the methodology by which that discovery was made. In his elaboration of psychoanalytic theory— and in this sense irrespective of his training in physiology and neurology—Freud does not begin by attempting to extend biology into the field of human psychology. Instead, he begins with a psychological theory that reaches "downward" to secure a biological grounding for the evidences of consciousness—evidences that, in the wake of Darwin, necessarily have their origin in an organic substrate.[8] How did this enterprise get its footing?

By the time Freud and Breuer published the *Studies on Hysteria* (1895), Freud had already formulated a psychological explanation of the nature and causation of neurosis. In most aspects that explanation, and the purely psychological evidences on which it is based, remained unchanged throughout the course of Freud's subsequent writings.[9] But when he first decided to attempt putting his psychological theories on a natural scientific footing, he turned to speculations on the mechanics and evolution of the body and nervous system to get his bearings. The result was the posthumously published draft that has come down to us as the "Project for a Scientific Psychology," written in 1895. The ambition of the "Project," Freud tells us,

> is to furnish a psychology that shall be a natural science: that is to rep-
> resent psychical processes as quantitatively determinate states of spe-
> cifiable material particles, thus making those processes perspicuous
> and free from contradiction. Two principal ideas are involved:
> (1) What distinguishes activity from rest is to be regarded as Q, subject
> to the general laws of motion. (2) Neurones are to be taken as the ma-
> terial particles.[10]

Even within the physio-neurological confines of the "Project," however, Freud felt the claims of the psychological field of phenomena
whose manifestations he was trying to explain. Thus we read that
"every psychological theory, apart from what it achieves from the
point of view of natural science, must fulfill yet another major re-
quirement. It should explain to us what we are aware of, in a most
puzzling fashion, through our consciousness."[11] Less explicitly, but
more decisively, the claims of Freud's point of departure in the phenomena of consciousness are recognized by the literalness with
which he pursues his intention of giving a material representation to
psychical processes. Thus, we soon learn that the "quantitative conception," i.e., "Q,"

> is derived directly from pathological clinical observation especially
> where excessively intense ideas were concerned—in hysterias and
> obsessions, in which, as we shall see, the quantitative characteristic
> emerges more plainly than in the normal. Processes such as stimulus,
> substitution, conversion and discharge, which had to be described
> there (in connection with those disorders), directly suggested the con-
> ception of neuronal excitation as quantity in a state of flow.[12]

By itself, this derivation of a material force from experienced psychological states seems to be nothing more than an early example of
Freud's recourse to "an objectivism that regresses immediately from
the level of self-reflection to contemporary positivism"[13]—an objectivism whose consequences Jürgen Habermas has given concise formulation to. But here Freud's epistemological leap is even cruder
than usual. For he presumes to infer the course of material "external" events in the nervous system directly from a train of inwardly
experienced (though outwardly expressed and observed) states of
consciousness. One cannot, of course, do this without running afoul
of the wearisome "mind–body" problem which, like the problem of

adding apples and oranges, is inherently insoluble since, as Descartes articulated the matter, the entities to be connected are defined from the outset to be incommensurable.

Nonetheless, Freud's direct derivation of "quantity in a state of flow" from the experience of "excessively intense ideas" signifies more than just a nineteenth-century positivist's presumption of the primary reality of material forces and entities. We must not forget that the material force inferred only *re*presents the psychical process—whose claim to epistemological priority in the articulation of Freud's scientific psychology is thereby asserted. This epistemological priority reveals its full meaning for the equally emphatic assertion of the body's existential primacy when we see where Freud finally carries the inference of "quantity in a state of flow" from the psychological experience of "excessively intense ideas." Freud carries that inference to the determination of a source for psychical energies—for "Q"—in the body. The rising of "endogenous quantities of excitation," we learn, along paths leading "from the interior of the body" to the neuronal cells of the nervous system constitutes "the *mainspring* of the psychical mechanism."[14] And a bit later we read, "it is thus that in the interior of the system there arises an impulsion which sustains all psychical activity. We know this power as will—the derivative of the *instincts* [Triebe]."[15]

The key matter that concerns us here is Freud's orientation of the body with respect to the mind as an interiority. The interiority that Freud invokes is traced by inference from the experience of excessively intense ideas to quantity in a state of flow, and from there to the interior of the body as the source from which the endogenous quantities arise. As such, it can never be reached by any technique of physiology or neurology. For this interiority is not the spatial inside of the body, observable upon dissection or surgical intervention. The "impulsion" that arises from the "interior of the system" signifies *the body lived from within*. Its evidences are the phenomena of consciousness themselves. And it is this fact that determines its appearance as an inwardness. This, then, is the meaning of the epistemological priority of the mind over and against the existential primacy of the body. In these formulations Freud posits the body as the origin and basis of the mind. And he does so because evolutionary science carries the unavoidable implication that human existence has an animal essence. The way in which Freud con-

strues this matter is to situate the body as the mind's ultimate inwardness. After Freud had abandoned the epistemologically
fallacious effort to derive material processes from physiological
ones, and had resolved to work only with psychological phenomena,
the situation of the body as the inward ground of mind remained.
Thus, in a typical formulation of the psychoanalytic period proper,
we read that "by an 'instinct' is provisionally to be understood the
psychical representative of an endosomatic, continuously flowing
source of stimulation, as contrasted with a 'stimulus', which is set up
by *single* excitations arising from *without*."[16] Now psychical phenomena take on the role of representing somatic stimuli. The instinct is a "psychical representative." But the situation of the body
as the ground of the mind's inwardness remains unchanged in this
reversal of roles.

Like Darwinian psychology, psychoanalysis is an instinct psychology—a psychology that refers the evidences of mind to the functions of organism. Freud uses the term *Trieb* (literally, "drive")
rather than *Instinkt* ("instinct" in the usual ethological sense) to indicate a more plastic notion. But in this he does not depart from the
usages of German mechanistic biology. "The zoologist," writes
antivitalist Heinrich Ernst Ziegler, "sees in the life of man many
drives *(Triebe)* whose root in the animal realm he can follow up-
wards."[17] Thus, Freud's use of the term *Trieb* is not decisive in distinguishing psychoanalysis from evolutionary psychology. The use
of the term *Trieb* does not make psychoanalysis any less (or, for that
matter, any more) biological in orientation. The decisive matter is
not the word Freud chooses to employ but his positing of the body
within the mind—his approach to organic reality from the "direction
of consciousness." Thus, in the preface to the third edition of the
Three Essays on the Theory of Sexuality—the book in which the
concept of instinct was first introduced into psychoanalytic theory—
we read, "my aim has . . . been to discover how far psychological investigation can throw light upon the biology of the sexual life of
man."[18] As Freud's close collaborator, Ferenczi, notes in his introduction to the Hungarian translation of that work, "Until now, the
possibility had never been contemplated that a psychological
method, and an 'introspective' one at that, could aid in the explanation of a biological problem."[19]

Psychoanalysis and the Framework of Dualism

Freud's attempt to approach the body through consciousness entails a fundamental difficulty. The problem is that the inward evidences available to introspection had already been staked out at the origins of modern science as describing a domain ontologically distinct from the outward domain occupied by the natural, material world to which the body belongs. I am referring, of course, to the dualism we have already mentioned: Descartes's bifurcation of reality into two independent and incommensurable substances. The *res cogitans*, Descartes tells us, consists in "a substance the whole nature or essence of which is to think, and that for its existence there is no need for any place, nor does it depend on any material thing."[20] With this distinction Descartes assigned a unique, if lonely, place to human existence within the vast but dead universe discovered by the new science of nature. Actualized in the mind's reflection on itself, the *res cogitans* secured for "consciousness" a realm distinct from the externality of nature. It thus served, in the words of E. A. Burtt, "to justify and atone for the reading of man and his interests out of nature."[21] What Burtt speaks of here is the deanthropomorphization process so starkly expressed by the other half of the dualism, where nature is stripped down to its bare bones. Its essence is mere extension.

Sigmund Freud still felt bound by this rudimentary articulation of the existent into two incommensurable domains of reality. Had not the whole history of scientific discovery culminating in Darwin's extraordinary feat confirmed its efficacy and truth? Yet Freud's postulation of the body as the inward ground of mind implicitly challenges the ground rules of understanding raised upon dualism. In positing the body (an object of external nature) as the ground of mind (the inward subject to which external nature appears), Freud tries to relocate the body within the dualistic framework of understanding. This is the outstanding characteristic of psychoanalytic theory. The peculiar situation of psychoanalytic theory in relation to Descartes's dualism is manifest in this philosophically naive but intuitively profound inversion of the body: the turning of the body outside in within the Cartesian framework.

But why do I say intuitively profound? From an epistemological standpoint, Freud's inversion would seem instead to express a fatal weakness in psychoanalytic theory—to bring into question in a most embarrassing fashion the scientific pretensions of psychoanalysis. Wherein lies the profundity I have claimed for it? The profundity of Freud's inversion is that it expresses a radical insight into the meaning of evolution for human self-understanding. It tries to express that insight, it is true, within a framework of thought that insight implicitly subverts. But, as we shall see, there was simply no other way to express that insight without leaving behind natural science and its impressive history of discovery entirely. Finally, Darwin himself opens the way to Freud's inversion of the body by implicitly altering the situation of understanding that dualism rested upon. In this way Freud's psychoanalysis turns out to be a response to the deeper resonances of Darwin's evolutionary biology for the framework of understanding whose rudimentary coordinates were articulated by Descartes. To grasp Freud's animating insight, we must render his relationship to Darwin transparent.

The path to the discovery of the connection between Freud and Darwin was cleared for me by the labors of Hans Jonas who, in his *Phenomenon of Life,* engages in an examination of "The Philosophical Aspects of Darwinism" as a preparatory movement for a philosophical biology. Let us, therefore, avail ourselves of Jonas's guidance across the slippery paths of ontology until we reach the point where we can take our leave and rejoin our consideration of Freud. We turn to the fifth and final section of Jonas's essay.

Darwinism and Dualism

"In one respect," Jonas begins, "the triumph which materialism achieved in Darwinism contains the germ of its own overcoming."[22] Jonas reminds us of "what made science fasten upon a certain form of dualism as the ontological setting most suitable for its purpose, entrench itself in its portion of the patrimony, and finally discard the other half as redundant."[23] What Jonas is referring to is the Cartesian distinction between the *res cogitans,* whose essential attribute is "awareness," and the *res extensa,* which is "untainted by the non-mathematical characters of being." Galileo, Jonas notes, "initiated the extrusion of undesirable features from physical reality." But

Descartes's dualism solved the problem of giving an account of these features by establishing a "dumping ground" for them wholly outside the natural world.

> The isolation of the *res cogitans* was the most effective way of securing the complete ontological detachment of external reality from what was not extended and measurable. Thus besides constituting this reality as a self-contained field for the universal application of mathematical analysis, the division provided the metaphysical justification for the all-out mechanical materialism of modern science.[24]

Jonas underscores here that "this justification lay in assigning the excluded, nonextended and therefore nonmechanical, characters a separate and fully acknowledged domain of their own, not in denying them reality." The justification for science's materialism lay in the ideality of the mind. "Alone with itself, materialism became an absurdity."[25]

Now, Darwinism, in accordance with its positivistic commitments, had managed "to credit the automatism of material nature with the generation of the branching and ascending life forms." But the "resulting monism also drew upon deserted matter the full weight of a burden from which [Cartesian] dualism had kept it free: that of having to account for the origins of *mind*."[26]

Jonas's point is not that science presumes to establish or found itself upon a metaphysics. The natural sciences do not concern themselves with a comprehension of the highest principles of being, in relation to which everything in the vast multiplicity of the existent finds its proper place. The sciences proceed by way of their own methods and research discrete object domains without being concerned about such ultimate questions. Nonetheless, "there are those among its own proper objects that force it to face the issue of materialism on the ontological level." Those objects are "living organisms, the mysterious meeting-place of Descartes' two substances, though he himself acknowledged such a 'meeting' in only one case."[27] That case was man. In contrast to his treatment of man, Descartes's theory of animal existence reduces animals to mere automata whose "functioning suggests to the human onlooker an inwardness analogous to his own *without their possessing any such inwardness*."[28] Man, partaking of both substances of the dualism, was the singular exception in a universe of unrelenting materiality.

Thus, at the cost of just one unmanageable metaphysical problem, the expurgation of the world of matter from the admixtures of mind was made defensible, since the claims of mind or inwardness were still honored by their allocation to a separate substance, with its independent set of phenomena under their own laws, even if the domain had to be contracted to the sphere of *human* consciousness.[29]

The success of the theory of evolution completely changed this situation, for it necessarily "abolished the special position of man which had warranted the Cartesian treatment of all the remainder."

The *continuity* of descent now established between man and the animal world made it impossible any longer to regard his mind, and mental phenomena as such, as the abrupt ingression of an ontologically foreign principle at just this point of the total flow. With the last citadel of dualism there also fell the isolation of man, and his own evidence became available again for the interpretation of that to which he belongs. For if it was no longer possible to regard his mind as discontinuous with prehuman biological history, then by the same token no excuse was left for denying mind, in proportionate degrees, to the closer or remoter ancestral forms, and hence to any level of animality: commonsense evidence was reinstated through the sophistication of theory—against its own spirit to be sure.[30]

The upshot of these matters is that "evolution undid Descartes' work more effectively than any metaphysical critique managed to" and that Darwinism "turns out to have been a thoroughly dialectical event." For "in the hour of the final triumph of materialism, the very instrument of it, 'evolution', implicitly transcended the terms of materialism and posed the ontological question anew—when it just seemed settled."[31]

It is here that we return to our consideration of Freudian theory. Jonas has brought us to the point where we can see the relation of the ontological situation arising out of Darwinism to Freud's inversion of the body within the framework of dualism—to the positing of the body as the ground of the within. For our purposes, the crucial aspect of Jonas's argument is his demonstration that, after Darwin's achievement, the evidences that now become available for the interpretation of nature are those pertaining to the inwardness of human experience. Freud's positing of the body as the inward ground of mind is a recognition of the same situation Jonas articulates, but responds to it in a different way. Because Darwin's nature is a nature with man in it, evolution means that the inwardness realized in the exercise of reflection becomes available for the interpretation of nature. The recognition of this situation is for Jonas the occasion for raising the ontological question anew—for bringing into question the nature of the existent in terms that stand *beyond* dualism. But, under the impact of Darwin's powerful *confirmation* of the efficacy of dualism through the discovery of the mechanisms that govern the development of organic life, the question can also take the form of how the appearance of mind in the domain of the *res extensa* could be comprehended—that is, how this new situation could be accounted for *within the framework of dualism*.

Psychoanalytic theory is a covert response to that question. The positing of the body within the mind adheres to the epistemological constraints of dualism while situating materiality as the basis of the subject. That is, Freud seeks to ground the evidence of human inwardness in the palpable evidence of human outwardness—the body. At the same time, Freud conducts this grounding operation by relying exclusively on the resources of internality, by reaching toward the body from the inside through reflection.

That after Darwin man appears within nature means by the same token that nature appears within man, not as a heteronomous force but as the very core of his being. Psychoanalysis tries to materialize a vision of human reality in these terms. The nature that appears within man is body. Psychoanalysis tries to think through the evidences of human experience to this ground. I mentioned before that Freud's thought struggles to express a radical insight into the meaning of evolution for human self-understanding, but within a framework that insight implicitly subverts. What I intend to demonstrate in the course of this study is that the tension signified by that fact governs the immanent movement of psychoanalytic thought.

The Ground Problem

Human existence has an animal essence. That is Darwin's lesson for mankind. But if that lesson is to be taken to heart, it must be worked out for human self-understanding. In the tradition of reflective philosophy, the thinking ego fixes on its own existence as the first and most fundamental certainty, the truth upon which all others are founded. Descartes's universal doubt, which finally locates a "fixed and immovable" Archimedean point[32] in the proposition "I think, therefore I am," is both the founding act and the exemplary instance of this tradition. For Descartes, the mind is its own first certainty.

If the lesson of Darwinism is to be worked out for the self-understanding, the first and most rudimentary consequence which must be taken into account is that the mind can no longer be understood to provide its own ground—to virtually stand under and support itself through the act of reflection. "Descartes' famous *Cogito ergo sum* applies no longer," declared Ernst Haeckel, a noted nineteenth-century German biologist and would-be philosopher of evolutionism; "It is just as easy to doubt or to deny the reality of my own consciousness as to doubt that of time and space."[33] Having discovered in its research and comprehension of the external world that it has its genesis therein, the mind loses faith in itself as the ground of its own reality and falls back upon the body, whose existential primacy is certified by evolutionary science. Freud's inversion of the body within the Cartesian framework—his positing of the body as the inward ground of mind—is a crude but incisive recognition of this rudimentary consequence of Darwinism for self-understanding.

However, in grasping that rudimentary consequence and articulating it to mean that all psychical activity is sustained by an impulsion arising from the interior of the body, that the mind is the body lived from within, Freud did not thereby materialize the meaning of evolution for self-understanding. Instead, what he did was to find a way of posing the issue within the framework of dualism. So articulated, the animal essence of human existence denotes a reality to which access must be gained through the gates of consciousness. What remained to be seen was whether this could be done—whether Freud could find a way to elucidate systematically the evidences of the analytic dialogue, and psychical phenomena in general, as the emanations of an organic substrate.

This task was by no means unproblematic, for it worked against the epistemological limitations of the framework in which it was posed. Epistemologically speaking, the reach of Freud's concepts could extend no further than the psychical phenomena generated in the movement of reflection. And the body, which he posited within the mind, ultimately lay external to the region of the existent that reflection marked off as its own reality. Given this limitation—a limitation decisive for the framework of dualism—how was Freud at the same time to make good his inversion of the body within that framework, his relocation of organic reality from the external to the internal domain? This is the question around which the whole movement of psychoanalytic theory turns. By materializing a vision of human being that compels the understanding, psychoanalytic theory must make good that relocation. If it does not, the psychoanalytic assumption that neurotic phenomena reflect the vicissitudes of an instinctual life proves illusory. And the psychoanalytic intention to provide a scientific self-understanding to men who know they are creaturely beings born of nature comes to naught. The theoretical vision frames the ultimate meaning of the practical activity, just as the practical activity forms the field of observation and verification for the theoretical framework. The problem of making good the positing of body as the ground of mind is Freud's ground problem, and let us note at the outset that the task it presents is unrealizable within the framework of dualism. Nonetheless, Freud finds ways to twist and bend that framework to suit his theoretical needs until the insight he seeks to express through it undermines its very foundations. That was not to happen, however, until Freud reached a moment of reckoning in *Totem and Taboo* (1912–13) which led him at last to the radical reformulations of *Beyond the Pleasure Principle* (1920). We have much distance to cover before we can deal with that part of our story.

We want to elucidate the immanent movement of thought by which Freud unfolds the task set by his ground problem—the problem of elaborating the purely psychological evidences of his phenomenal field so as to secure the body as their ground. Freud articulates the dimensions of this task in condensed form in a letter to Wilhelm Fleiss, his close intellectual companion in the critical period between his self-analysis and the completion of *The Interpretation of Dreams* (1900). In the letter of March 10, 1898, Freud complains of the inadequacy of his purely psychological explanation of dreams.

> It seems to me as though the theory of wish-fulfilment has only brought the psychological solution and not the biological, or rather, metapsychical one. (I am going to ask you seriously, by the way, whether I may use the name of metapsychology for my psychology that leads behind consciousness.) Biologically, dream life seems to me to derive entirely from the residues of the prehistoric period of life (between ages of one and three)—the same period which is the source of

the unconscious and also contains the aetiology of all the psychoneuroses, the period normally characterized by an amnesia analogous
to hysterical amnesia.[34]

In this statement Freud captures in a single breath, as it were, the
dimensions of the task set for him by his ground problem. Metapsychology[35] signifies a reality both beyond and more fundamental than
the psychological domain. That reality is first and foremost biology.
But, at the same time, metapsychology means the "psychology that
leads behind consciousness"—i.e., the psychology of the unconscious. Metapsychology thus has two aspects, of which biology is the
more fundamental, since it is the source of the unconscious. But biology is not metapsychological in the absolute sense of denoting an
external reality separated from the mind by an unbreachable hiatus.
Metapsychologically speaking, biology refers to a "prehistoric period of life"—to infantile experiences later covered over by an
amnesia.

The coining of the term *metapsychology* is provocative. Signify-
ing both a reality behind psychology (the unconscious) and a reality
beyond, though not discontinuous with psychology (biology),
metapsychology expresses the tension created by the ground problem—by the positing of the body within the mind without abandoning the epistemological constraints of dualism. By denoting both
"biology" and "the unconscious," metapsychology marks out the dimensions of the groundwork Freud will lay down in accordance
with the imperatives of the ground problem. Since the unconscious
has its origin in the biological vicissitudes of an infantile prehistory,
"biology" and "the unconscious" are ultimately two coordinate aspects of a single metapsychological reality. But their disposition
with respect to the bodily ground is not the same. The infantile prehistory is biology because it is closer to the body in its unaccultur-
ated originality, while the unconscious remains closer to consciousness and its contemporarily lived manifestations.

The infantile prehistory thus gains an existential primacy from its
closeness to the body, while the unconscious gains an epistemological priority from its closeness to the psychical field of phenomena.
The laying out of the groundwork necessarily follows the order of
epistemological priority. The unfolding of the task set by the ground
problem thus does not work from the ground up but from the surface
downward. Freud begins with that aspect closest to the field of phe-

nomena in order to reach that aspect closest to the bodily ground. This tension between phenomena and ground accounts for the peculiar dynamic in the development of Freud's thought. Thus, as he writes Fleiss just after the completion of *The Interpretation of Dreams:*

Mental apparatus. φ [perception]	Curious things are at work in the
Hysteria-clinical	bottom storey. A sexual theory
Sexual-organic	may be the immediate successor
	to the dream book.[36]

Together, the "dream-book" *(The Interpretation of Dreams)* and the "sexual theory" *(Three Essays on the Theory of Sexuality)* constitute the diphasic laying down of the groundwork of psychoanalytic understanding in accordance with the requirements of the ground problem. Beginning at the "top storey" with the appearances of consciousness, Freud opens up a depth dimension in psychical life by establishing a psychology of the unconscious through the interpretation of dreams. The *Three Essays on the Theory of Sexuality,* published five years after the dream book, then anchor those depths in the (pre)historic vicissitudes of the sexual instinct. Like psychoanalytic therapy itself, psychoanalytic theory unfolds backward toward its ground. The *psychology of the unconscious* and the *theory of psychosexual development* work out in two separate phases the task set by the ground problem. We noted before that these two aspects are coordinate, but with different dispositions toward the bodily ground. We shall thus consider them separately before we examine how they fit together to describe a single metapsychological reality. We must never forget, however, that in the articulation of the one, the presence of the other is already implied. Even though the dream book and the sexual theory were published five years apart, they in fact, as Ernest Jones informs us, "had been worked out together."[37]

CHAPTER 3

The Grounding Operation

The Starting Point: Studies on Hysteria

Our interest is in how Freud lays the foundations of the psychoanalytic perspective—that is, in how Freud materializes a novel vision of human reality in the wake of Darwin's determination that human existence has an animal essence. The materialization of that vision, however, operates within a preestablished framework of understanding—the framework of Cartesian dualism. What makes psychoanalysis, nonetheless, a radical venture is that Freud inverts the body within that framework by turning the body outside in within it. If this is the case, the side of the framework marked out as its own by the thinking ego—the domain of the *res cogitans*—must betray the impact of this inversion. That indeed it does is patent in the distance Freud traveled between the *Studies on Hysteria* (1895), his major statement of the prepsychoanalytic period, and *The Interpretation of Dreams* and the *Three Essays on the Theory of Sexuality*, the founding works of the psychoanalytic perspective.

The psychology of the *Studies*, which Freud coauthored with Joseph Breuer, is not a psychology of the unconscious. Nor is the therapeutic method described in it psychoanalysis as such. Breuer and Freud christened it the cathartic method. How did the cathartic method develop into psychoanalysis, and what is the significance of that development? Freud's 1908 preface to the *Studies* provides some answers. "The attentive reader will be able to detect in the present book," Freud tells us, "the germs of all that has since been added to the theory of catharsis: for instance, the part played by sexual factors and infantilism, the importance of dreams and of unconscious symbolism."[1] It is surely no coincidence that the two kinds of

"additions" to the theory of catharsis Freud offers by way of example
correspond to the two facets of psychoanalytic theory we have identified as constituting the groundwork of psychoanalytic understanding—the theory of psychosexual development ("sexual factors and
infantilism") and the psychology of the unconscious ("the importance of dreams and of unconscious symbolism"). Clearly, what
came to Freud's mind in writing this preface was what distinguished psychoanalysis definitively from the earlier cathartic theory. What is decisive for us, and what I shall demonstrate in what
follows, is that while the theory of catharsis presented in the *Studies*
contains the germs of psychoanalytic theory, Freud does not develop them into psychoanalysis merely by explicating the ego-centered logic that inheres in the theory of catharsis. Nor are the basic
assumptions of the psychoanalytic period—that the unconscious is
the basis of mental life and that neurotic phenomena reflect the vicissitudes of an instinctual life history—themselves necessary inferences from what appears in the *Studies*. Psychoanalytic theory is
truly *added* to the theory of catharsis in order to yield psychoanalytic therapy. That is to say, the theoretical vision frames the ultimate
meaning of the practical activity.

But what of the germs of that theoretical vision Freud says are already found in the clinically bound formulations of the *Studies?* Am
I saying that psychoanalytic theory arises independently of and in
isolation from the context of Freud's clinical activities? Not at all. On
the contrary, the analytic dialogue provides the irreplaceable means
for the investigation and empirical demonstration both of the unconscious and of the role of psychosexual factors.[2] Nevertheless, the
framework in which psychoanalysis fixes the facts of clinical observation and investigation is not the one immanent to the dialogic exchange that characterizes the cathartic period. Psychoanalytic theory is not structured by the immanent teleology of the ego which
governs that exchange. Instead, the framework provided by the psychology of the unconscious and the theory of psychosexual development *inverts* the reflective, ego-centered logic inherent in that
exchange and, in the process, *occludes* the ego. The absence of an
ego concept in the founding works of psychoanalytic theory is thus
no oversight on Freud's part. Nor can it be explained away with the
assertion that Freud chose to defer consideration of the ego until he
had completed his investigation of the unconscious. The occlusion

of the ego is the *conditio sine qua non* for the founding of the psychoanalytic perspective and reflects Freud's inversion of the body within the framework of dualism—the twisting and bending of that framework in order to express the meaning of evolution for human self-understanding.

Our purpose in turning to the theory of catharsis, then, is to show how, in the movement to the psychoanalytic period proper, Freud subordinates therapy to theory. In laying the groundwork of psychoanalytic understanding, Freud found in the clinical phenomena explored during the cathartic period the essential clues. But Freud's rendering of those phenomena as the signs of a metapsychological reality is explainable only by the fact that in the psychoanalytic period he felt himself to be standing in the covert but ubiquitous presence of the body. As we shall see, Freud inverts the reflective, ego-centered logic of the early analytic method and occludes the ego, just in order to express the metapsychological reality.

According to the *Studies*, hysteria has its basis in the "splitting of consciousness." This splitting is provoked by a traumatic event. In the traumatic moment the ego repudiates any idea incompatible with it.

> When this process occurs for the first time there comes into being a nucleus and center of crystallization for the formation of a psychical group divorced from the ego—a group around which everything which would imply an acceptance of the incompatible idea subsequently collects.[3]

In the outbreak of hysteria, these split-off psychical phenomena return to manifest themselves symbolically as physical dysfunctions or behavioral compulsions that the subject does not understand and over which he has no control. The analytic dialogue aims to free the subject from his symptoms through the interpretative disclosure of their hidden meaning.

The genesis of the subject's symptoms in the repression of ideas incompatible with the ego was not itself an immediate, direct clinical observation. Rather it was inferred from the course of the therapy and its outcome. What justified and even necessitated that inference was the observation that

> each individual hysterical symptom immediately and permanently disappeared when we had succeeded in bringing clearly to light the memory of the event by which it was provoked and in arousing its ac-

companying affect, and when the patient had described that event in
the greatest possible detail and had put the affect into words.[4]

The therapeutic activity consists in the progressive restoration to
consciousness—along with the accompanying affects—of disowned
provinces of experience that the patient resists allowing into the
transparent web of his thoughts. The process ends when the work of
interpretation has succeeded in uncovering the original traumatic
moment, thereby "compelling the psychical group that had been
split off to unite once more with the ego-consciousness."[5] At that
point the hysterical symptoms, which had cryptically encoded the
contents of the split-off psychical group, disappear. The unity and
integrity of the ego are restored.

The simultaneous disappearance of hysterical symptoms and
coming to appearance of memories associated with them required
Breuer and Freud to postulate the working of psychical processes
behind the back of consciousness. "We must presume . . . that the
psychical trauma—or more precisely the memory of the trauma—
acts like a foreign body which long after its entry must continue to
be regarded as an agent that is still at work."[6] Thus, as the authors
conclude in their famous dictum, *"Hysterics suffer mainly from
reminiscences."*[7]

The Psychology of the Unconscious

The theory of hysteria, drawing on material exclusively from clinical
evidences and making only such inferences as are necessary to
make sense of those evidences, predicates the existence of unconscious psychical processes—processes that the hysterical symptoms
symbolically enshrine. Does this theory, then, provide the basis for
the articulation of the psychology of the unconscious? The answer is
no.

The theory found in the *Studies on Hysteria* is an inadequate basis for the articulation of a psychology of the unconscious because
everything about it points to the primacy of consciousness. In
Breuer's contributions this is explicit. But even Freud, who otherwise self-consciously left the question open in this period,[8] shows
his ambivalence about the status of the unconscious in the *Studies*
by his occasional use of the term "subconscious" in its place.[9] The
term subconscious implies a psychical state *inferior* to that of consciousness. In *The Interpretation of Dreams* Freud explicitly re-

pudiates the term for a reason that is highly revealing: "Such a distinction seems precisely calculated to stress the equivalence of what is psychical with what is conscious."[10] This equivalence is precisely what the psychology of the unconscious must negate. In *The Interpretation of Dreams* Freud for the first time makes that negation with the assertion that "the unconscious is the true psychical reality."[11] In contrast, the removal of hysterical symptoms through the cathartic method allows for the assignation of psychical status to unconscious contents only in the wake of their reintegration into the unity of ego consciousness. In the *Studies* Freud admits that his observations concerning unconscious processes are made only by regarding psychical phenomena "from the position we are able to assume after recovery for the purpose of surveying the case as a whole."[12] And later we read, "It is clearly impossible to say anything . . . about the state which the pathogenic material was in before the analysis—until we have arrived at a thorough clarification of our basic psychological views, especially on the nature of consciousness."[13]

This clarification, when it finally comes in the dream book, is made on the basis of metapsychological considerations. Freud no doubt found it suggestive that in reconstructing the logic of hysteria in the wake of its resolution, he could see "the peaks of the trains of thought dipping down into the unconscious—the reverse of what has been asserted of our normal psychical processes."[14] But the very fact that the inverted structure of such trains of thought represents a *pathological* formation prevented Freud from using it as the model for normal psychical processes. Indeed, the dipping of the peaks of trains of thought into the unconscious is itself the pathology that the cathartic method seeks to set aright. Nothing in the psychological evidences of the early analytic period permits Freud to assign to consciousness a status subordinate to unconsciousness. On the contrary, the logic of the analytic dialogue in cathartic treatment affirms the primacy of consciousness. Let us come to a closer understanding of why this is so.

The analysis begins, let us remember, not with the splitting off of conscious contents, with repression, but with the *return* of the repressed. The analyst encounters the unconscious only as a manifestation of discontinuity in consciousness—a manifestation which the hysterical symptom just *is*. This manifestation of discontinuity conceals an unconscious content at the same moment that it discloses its existence. Upon interpretation (in which the subject himself has participated), the hysterical symptom dissolves and is replaced by a memory that takes up its appropriate place in the continuity of the subject's life history. The hysterical symptom thus stands as a negative moment in the self-explication of the ego—an "unconscious" moment whose determinate relations with the rest of consciousness resist elucidation.

In searching for and trying to bring to consciousness the memory that the symptom symbolically represents, the analyst is guided by the appearance of "gaps and imperfections" in the patient's consciousness.[15] For these gaps and imperfections indicate the location of the logical relations that have been withdrawn from consciousness. By seizing on these lacunae, the analyst enters into the "depths" of the patient's mind—depths that lay concealed behind the self-consistent unity of surface consciousness. In the final chapter of the *Studies*, which Freud authored alone, we read:

> We must get hold of a piece of the logical thread, by whose guidance alone we may hope to penetrate to the interior. We cannot expect that the free communications made by the patient, the material from the most superficial strata, will make it easy for the analyst to recognize at what points the path leads into the depths or where he is to find the starting-points of the connections of thought of which he is in search. On the contrary; This is precisely what is carefully concealed; the account given by the patient sounds as if it were complete and self-contained.[16]

The way into the interior depths is approached peripherally, through the finding of a piece of logical thread in the interstices of the patient's free associations, in the breaks and silences of his communications with the analyst.

The problem is that once the work of interpretation is done, the patient's resistances overcome, and the connections concealed in the "depths" made transparent, we are thrown back again to the "surface" of consciousness. The overcoming of pathology coincides with the restoration of transparent and determinate relations that link the psychical contents of the mind into a unity. The therapeutic process carries us only so far into the depths as the original traumatic moment, at which point the patient, in his affectively charged recognition of that moment, is released from his symptoms. The split-off psychical group is fully reunited with ego consciousness. The psychology of the *Studies* is, at bottom, an ego psychology, for the unconscious is nothing but a pathological deformation in the structure of the ego.

Two fundamental features distinguish the characterization of unconscious mental processes in *The Interpretation of Dreams* from their characterization in the *Studies*. First, the unconscious becomes substantive. No longer identified merely with the pathological distortion of normal mental processes, the unconscious becomes a constituent component of the mind as such. Second, the unconscious displaces the conscious to become the "true psychical reality." In these two propositions the psychology of the unconscious comes authentically into being.

The first of these propositions was reached by the "royal road" of dream interpretation, a road opened up to Freud in the course of his clinical encounters. Freud found that the technique for interpreting dissociated psychical phenomena could be applied with equal effectiveness to be unintelligible, marginal mental formations of dream life. It was "in the course" of his "psycho-analytic studies," Freud tells us in the dream book, "that I came upon dream-interpretation."

> My patients were pledged to communicate to me every idea or thought that occurred to them in connection with some particular subject; amongst other things, they told me their dreams and so taught me that a dream can be inserted into the psychical chain that has to be traced backwards in the memory from a pathological idea. It was then only a short step to treating the dream itself as a symptom and to applying to dreams the method of interpretation that had been worked out for symptoms.[17]

As a universally experienced "symptom" of unconscious mental processes, the dream became a vehicle for making the unconscious a constituent component of mental life. As we read in the *Introductory Lectures,*

> dreams are themselves a neurotic symptom which, moreover, offer us the priceless advantage of occurring in all healthy people. Indeed, supposing all human beings were healthy, so long as they dreamt we could arrive from their dreams at almost all the discoveries which the investigation of the neuroses has led to.[18]

The depths that open up to the analyst in the exploration of psychical pathology and close to him again in its cure thus became available universally in the investigation of the images of sleep.

The second fundamental feature of the psychology of the unconscious radicalizes the assertion that unconscious mental processes are a universal component of the mind. The psychology of the unconscious is secured definitively in the further assertion that appears for the first time in the dream book—the assertion that the unconscious is the true psychical reality. The *Introductory Lectures* offer a particularly clear discussion of this point.

> Psycho-analysis declares that mental processes are in themselves unconscious and that of all mental life it is only certain individual acts and portions that are conscious . . . we are in the habit of identifying what is psychical with what is conscious. We look upon consciousness as nothing more or less than the *defining* characteristic of the psychical, and psychology as the study of the contents of consciousness. . . . Yet psycho-analysis cannot avoid raising this contradiction; it cannot accept the identity of the conscious and the mental.

Freud concludes this discussion with the striking assertion that "the hypothesis of there being unconscious mental process paves the way to a decisive new orientation in the world and in science."[19]

It is one thing to assert the universal existence of unconscious mental processes and quite another to assert that mental processes are "in themselves" unconscious. Nothing about dream life provides the grounds for the latter assertion. To dissociate the mental and the conscious in this radical sense of making the latter a derivative, secondary aspect of the former is a matter of no small moment. For it signifies the *inversion* of the relationship between the conscious and the unconscious encountered in the as yet theoretically untutored therapeutic activity. My argument is that this inversion can be understood only in terms of Freud's positing of the body as the metapsychological basis of mind. In Freud the body becomes the transcendental guide for elaborating the domain of inwardness. What appear in consciousness are the phenomenal manifestations of a reality that "in itself" is not conscious. That reality is the body. And suggestive here is Freud's allusion in the dream book to another transcendental empiricist, Immanuel Kant, in that section where the primacy of the unconscious is unequivocally affirmed. "The unconscious is the true psychical reality; in its innermost nature it is as much unknown to us as the reality of the external world, and it is as incompletely presented by the data of consciousness as is the external world by the communications of our sense organs."[20]

In the wake of Darwin and man's appearance within nature, the understanding makes recourse to the appearance of nature within man as the basis of his own most intimate evidences. The first rudimentary consequence of evolution for self-understanding is that the mind can no longer be considered to constitute its own ground through the movement of reflection. Its ground is body. Freud tries to reach that ground through the evidences of consciousness by inverting the body within the framework of dualism—by positing the body within the mind. This inversion is manifest in the first phase of the laying of the groundwork of psychoanalytic understanding through the inversion of the relation between conscious and unconscious as that relation stands in the analytic dialogue. The early cathartic method in essence subordinates the unconscious to the teleology of consciousness, which finds its ultimate expression in the completed movement of self-reflection that successful catharsis entails.

In positing the body as the ground of mind, Freud inverts that relationship. When looked at from the standpoint of the tradition of reflective thought, this amounts to dissolving the reflectively generated unity of the mind and releasing psychical contents from their grounding therein. In other words, the psychology of the unconscious, by preparing psychical contents for the somatic grounding Freud desires to provide the mind, must be raised upon the ruins of the sovereignty of the ego. The securing of "depth" as a constituent coordinate of psychical existence through the discovery of unconscious processes in dreams makes an important advance upon the conditions obtaining in the analytic dialogue which, as we have seen, constantly throws us back to the surface of consciousness. In adding a topographical dimension to the mind, Freud at the same time opposes a dark depth to the transparent surface that the ego realizes in its reflective self-explication. Not surprisingly, the very notion of an ego is absent from *The Interpretation of Dreams*. Instead, Freud speaks merely of consciousness, whose role is reduced to that of a passive receptor to psychical events that transpire outside its domain. "But what part is there left," he asked rhetorically, "to be played in our scheme by consciousness, which was once so omnipotent and hid all else from view? *Only that of a sense-organ for the perception of psychical qualities.*"[21]

The Theory of Psychosexual Development

In the inversion that founds the psychology of the unconscious, the psychical contents held together by the mind's transparency to itself are released from their determinate and transparent relations within the reflectively constituted unity of the ego and resolved back into psychical "raw material," as Freud calls it. This inversion constitutes the first phase of the grounding operation. In the second phase this "raw material" is reconstituted in conformity with a new logic—not the grammatical logic generated by the self-explication of the ego but the logic of psychosexual development, a logic governed by the historical vicissitudes of the body. The two phases of the groundwork of psychoanalytic understanding represent this new logic, but not with the same immediacy. The psychology of the unconscious, being closer to the phenomenal field (consciousness) and further from the ground (body), represents the essential temporality of this logic *mediately* as a concrescence of past and present within a topographical articulation of surface and depth. Note how Freud presents matters in 1913:

> in spite of all later development that occurs in the adult, none of the infantile mental formations perish. All the wishes, instinctual impulses, modes of reaction and attitudes of childhood are still demonstrably present in maturity and in appropriate circumstances can emerge once more. *They are not destroyed but merely overlaid—to use the spatial mode of description which psycho-analytic psychology has been obliged to adopt.* Thus it is part of the nature of the mental past that, unlike the historic past, it is not absorbed by its derivative; it persists (whether actually or only potentially) alongside what has proceeded from it. [my italics][22]

We have seen how this topographical "spatial mode" develops out of the analytic dialogue while inverting its reflective, ego-centered logic. *The Interpretation of Dreams* fixes that inversion in a new framework for the understanding of mental life in which the unconscious is the true psychical reality. The second phase of the grounding operation, executed in the *Three Essays on the Theory of Sexuality*, elaborates that new logic in its temporal mode. This temporal mode, the more fundamental of the two, also develops out of the analytic dialogue. And, not surprisingly, it too takes shape through an inversion of the teleological, ego-centered structure of that dialogue. Let us see how.

We shall not have to look far to discover the germs, already present in the *Studies,* from which the theory of psychosexual development grew. For the depths behind the surface of consciousness to which analysis penetrates represent at the same time a backward reach through time. Hysterical symptoms have a history and take on significance in a biographical context. The case history of a hysterical neurosis reveals "an intimate connection between the story of the patient's sufferings and the symptoms of his illness."[23] In the construction of a case history each neurotic "theme" is found to form a "file of memories" whose contents "always emerge in a chronological order." These chronologically ordered, thematically classified mnemonic "files," however, are not produced by the subject in story form. Rather, these files

> make the work of analysis more difficult by the peculiarity that, in re-
> producing memories, they reverse the order in which these originated.
> The freshest and newest experience in the file appears first, as an outer
> cover, and last of all comes the experience with which the series in fact
> began.[24]

The reverse appearance of relevant memories (i.e., symptoms and their narrative biographical context) in the course of the therapy does not itself, however, get to the heart of the matter. More critical is the fact that the further back into the past the analysis reaches, the deeper it penetrates into the unconscious repressed material and the closer it gets to the "pathogenic idea" in "its purest manifestation"—to the original traumatic moment.[25] Thus, commenting on the "reversed course" the analysis followed in the case of Miss Lucy R., Freud notes, "I have had the same experience in a whole number of cases; the symptoms that had arisen later masked the earlier ones, and the key to the whole situation lay in the last symptoms to be reached by the analysis."[26]

Thus the hysterical symptoms in their contemporary manifestations represent the continuing activity of the past in the present, while at the same time they conceal the meaning of that past. In the language of Freud's later *Papers on Technique,* in the subject's symptoms he repeats a past he cannot remember.[27] Guided by the memory of his sufferings, the subject recovers the contents of a banished past by discovering its connections to an inwardly grasped life history. The bringing to consciousness of repressed psychical contents and their reunification with ego consciousness is thus at the same time the recollection of a forgotten history, the key to whose systematic obscuration lies in the original traumatic moment. The transformation of symptoms into memories is crucial to the existential sense that psychoanalysis materializes. The analysis realizes the self as a temporally conditioned entity in the simultaneous release of the subject from the past as contemporary compulsion and the restoration to the subject of the past as the transparent continuity of experience through time.

The realization of a temporally conditioned self in catharsis is fully compatible with the ego-centered logic of reflection arising out of Cartesianism. In the *Studies* the analysis of hysterical symptoms carries the reflective recollection back only as far as the specifics of the pathology demand—namely, to the experiential instance that forms the pathogenic nucleus of the neurosis—in order to fill the gaps in memory that corrupt the textual coherence and integrity of the ego. The movement of remembrance is the process of the ego's self-formation.

In order to demonstrate how the logic of psychosexual development inverts the temporal dimension of the analytic dialogue, and in the process shatters the sovereignty of the ego, I shall engage Habermas's treatment of Freud's developmental theory. Because Habermas thinks that psychoanalytic theory is rooted in the logic of reflection, his treatment serves as a foil for the understanding I wish to advance. For Habermas, the developmental theory of the psychoanalytic period proper merely extends the recollection process described in the *Studies* by providing a systematic framework for the resolution of psychical life into a complete sequence of temporally linked configurations. This more radical temporalization remains subordinate, however, to the logic of the ego's self-reflective constitution. Indeed, Habermas claims for the ego-id-superego theory of Freud's later thought the role of providing a theoretical formalization of the ego's self-formative process under which its narrative developmental history is subsumed. With the aid of the structural model, the subject's developmental history "is represented schematically as a self-formative process that goes through various stages of self-objectivation and that has its telos in the self-consciousness of a reflectively appropriated life-history."[28] "The final state of a self-formative process is attained only if the subject remembers its identifications and alienations, the objectivations forced upon it and the reflections it arrived at, as the path upon which it constituted itself."[29]

This interpretation of the relation of psychoanalytic theory to the analytic activity draws on the radical reformulations that constitute Freud's later ego psychology. Its effect is to obviate the *occlusion* of the ego, which is definitive in the founding of the psychoanalytic perspective. As we shall see, however, Habermas is also wrong in his treatment of Freud's ego psychology. The ego of Freud's final theory is not the transparent ego of the *Studies*. It is a resurrected ego which bears all the marks of its trials at Golgotha. In order to see what is at stake in my disagreement with Habermas, we must turn to the work of Wilhelm Dilthey (1833–1911), which Habermas himself uses to facilitate his interpretation. Since Dilthey's intellectual project—the critique of historical reason—led him to realize the relations of reflection and temporality, it can serve to illuminate critical aspects of Freud's analytic dialogue and the meaning psychoanalytic theory brings to it. By way of contrast, Dilthey will put us in a position to see how the addition of infantilism and psychosexual factors to the theory of catharsis inverts rather than completes the ego-centered teleology of self-reflection and how the theory of psychosexual development, which brings these additions to the analytic dialogue, fixes that inversion in accordance with the requirements of the ground problem—with the positing of the somatic ground. In seeing this, we shall also see clearly how the body is brought to bear within the domain of phenomena opened up by reflection as the metapsychological guide for laying the foundations of psychoanalytic theory.

We begin our consideration of Dilthey with his determination of "life" as the fundamental reality. "Every expression of life has a meaning insofar as it is a sign which expresses something that is a part of life. Life does not mean anything other than itself. There is nothing in it which points to a meaning beyond it."[30] We need not hesitate, I think, to read these words for their religious bearing. The cumulative testimony of thinkers in the nineteenth century to the disappearance of a transcendent source of meaning is too overwhelming for us to doubt the true weight of Dilthey's words. Certainly for the man still possessed of metaphysical perceptions, life is veritably filled with signs that point beyond life. For Dilthey, the understanding, denied access to a meaning beyond life, makes recourse to whatever meaning may be found within it. And, given the unsurpassability of life, it is not surprising that for Dilthey "the category of meaning belongs to memory"[31] and the meaning found within life lies in the recollection of life itself. In Dilthey, the recollection of life occupies the realm of inwardness that reason's self-reflection grounds in Descartes and whose infrastructure is developed to its limits in Hegelian philosophy. "Life in its totality," Dilthey notes, ". . . takes the place of Hegel's 'Reason.' "[32]

> Life is the fundamental fact which must form the starting point for philosophy. It is that which is known from within, that behind which we cannot go. Life cannot be brought before the judgement seat of reason.[33]

What is given in the fundamental fact of life is nothing but time itself. "Life is something temporal,"[34] and, concomitantly, "Man is something historical."[35]

> Life seen as a temporal succession of events which affect each other is historical life. It is only possible to grasp it through the reconstruction of the course of events in a memory which produces, not the particular event but the system of connections and the stages of its development.[36]

Finally, Dilthey roots the possibility of historical understanding—for this is the systematic intention of his thought—in the most fundamental context in which this system of connections appears, and that is the course of an individual life. "Autobiography is the highest and most instructive form in which the understanding of life confronts us."[37] The understanding of others, of the institutions, artifacts, and texts that express their lives, and hence the understanding of history itself, is founded on self-understanding. "The power and breadth of our own lives and the energy with which we reflect on them are the foundations of historical vision. It alone enables us to give life back to the bloodless shadows of the past."[38] In the recollected course of an individual life "we have the germinal cell of history, for here the specific historical categories arise."[39] Succinctly put, man "understands history because he himself is a historical being."[40]

Significantly in the context of our concerns, the temporal nature of existence that appears when life, denied a meaning beyond itself, falls back on itself to recollect its experience through time is nonetheless founded for Dilthey upon the category of identity.

> Because the sequence of a life is held together by the consciousness of identity, all the moments of that life have their foundation in the category of identity. The discrete is linked into continuity; by following the lines of meaning from the small figure of childhood living for the moment, to the man who maintains his firm resolute inner life in the face of the world, we can relate the succession of influences and reactions to something which is shaping itself and which, thus, develops as something inwardly determined.[41]

The category of identity stabilizes the temporality that the recollection of life realizes. Consciousness of identity masters all accidents and incidents of life and discovers in the "succession of influences and reactions" the emergence of an inwardly determined, resolutely maintained self. As with Leibniz's monads, which Dilthey invokes at one point in a slightly different context,[42] nothing extraneous intervenes or intrudes upon the smooth surface of this identity. The temporality it realizes forms a closed circle of transparent moments that begins and ends with the consciousness of identity that holds the moments together in their contemporaneous unity.

We turned to a consideration of Dilthey in order to demonstrate what is at stake in our disagreement with Habermas's subsumption of the temporality realized in the analytic dialogue under the schematic of the ego's self-realization, formalized, according to Habermas, in the structural model of Freud's later theory. Dilthey provides a kind of pure case in which temporality is both realized and contained within·the bounds of an ego-centered exercise in reflection. The condition for that realization is the consciousness of identity that holds the sequence of a life together. Resoluteness is all that maintains this consciousness. A virtual will-to-identity replaces the rational infrastructure realized by an earlier generation in the positing of the self through reason and reason through the self.

Freudian analysis in its early cathartic form differs from the reflective movement described by Dilthey in that it begins, not with the consciousness of identity, but with the dissociation of consciousness. Yet this in itself is not decisive insofar as an immanent teleology informs both Dilthey's recollection of life story and Freud's restoration of a distorted past into the continuity of ego consciousness. The only difference is that the "consciousness of identity" which stands at the *outset* of Dilthey's autobiographical recollection makes its appearance at the *outcome* of the analytic dialogue. In Freud, the ego undergoes a transformation in the process of healing a traumatic wound it has suffered, whereas Dilthey's ego simply makes explicit what implicitly it already is. In both cases the ego is at once the subject and object of a logic of reflection.[43] In the founding of the psychoanalytic perspective, however, Freud inverts the ego-centered logic of the *Studies*. The addition of infantilism and psychosexual factors to the cathartic method subordinates the teleology of the ego to the "archeology" (to use Paul Ricoeur's term) of psychical origination. As Freud put it in 1917, psychoanalytic science constitutes a blow to the narcissism of the ego.[44] A comparison with Dilthey illustrates how this is so.

Let us note that the interpretative logic of the therapeutic process differs from that of Dilthey's autobiographical recollection in its direction. Dilthey follows the "lines of meaning" forward from the small figure of childhood living for the moment to the resolute, inwardly determined man—which is to say, in a progressive movement from the past to the present. In the cathartic period, on the other hand, reflection moves regressively from the present to the past and reaches a climax in the disclosure of an original traumatic moment. Nonetheless, a unified ego is the outcome of both processes.

The theory of psychosexual development models itself on the regressive movement of the cathartic method. The addition of infantilism and psychosexual factors to the theory of catharsis signifies a carrying of this regressive movement ever backward to the earliest experiences. Psychoanalysis "consists in tracing back one psychical structure to another which preceded it in time and out of which it developed."[45] This backward reach does not stop, however, at the earliest consciously available memories but claims to penetrate behind them to an infantile prehistory which has been covered over by an amnesia. It does this "along the path of instinctual activity,"[46] using the experiences arising out of the biological function of sexuality as its guiding thread. Sexual experiences would seem perfectly suited to this task, not only because they are undeniably linked to human biology but also because they possess a certain density that resists complete reflective elucidation. In tracing instinctual configurations back to the earliest "experiences" of infantile existence, psychoanalysis claims to discover the decisive "fixations" through which the whole subsequent development of the subject must be read. Just as in the theory of catharsis the traumatic moment persists behind all later transformations, so in psychoanalytic theory proper the original prehistorical configuration of instinctual impulses is definitive for the ontogeny of psychical life as such.

We saw earlier how the psychology of the unconscious radicalizes the theory of catharsis by making the unconscious a universal component of the mind. Correlatively, the theory of psychosexual development universalizes the significance of psychobiographical moments, which are defined, moreover, in instinctual terms. What one experiences as an infant is a contingency. That those experiences are definitive is not. At the same time, we saw how the psychology of the unconscious inverts the relation of conscious and unconscious as that relation stands in the analytic dialogue. The subordination of surface to depth in that case has its correlate in the determinative significance of the past for the present in the case of the theory of psychosexual development. The metapsychological presence of the body as a theoretical proposition and not the logic of the analytic dialogue as a therapeutic practice grounds that determination. The theory of psychosexual development inverts the teleological structure of the analytic dialogue by stretching the recollection of experience back from contemporary consciousness to an infantile prehistory and fixing it there for the recognition of the self. In the process, the ego in its contemporary configuration is subordinated to the prereflective, biological strivings of the infant that lie at its core. Psychosexuality opens a wound in the ego that reflection can never heal.

It is true that in the later development of an ego psychology, after 1914, Freud ascribes a synthetic function to the ego, thus seeming to root his ego concept in the ego-centered logic of reflection described in the *Studies*. Thus, in 1919 we read that

> the neurotic patient presents us with a torn mind, divided by resistances. As we analyze it and remove the resistances, it grows together; the great unity which we call his ego fits into itself all the instinctual impulses which before had been split off and held apart from it.[47]

Habermas, whose interpretation draws on the later Freud, cites this passage as evidence that "analytic knowledge is self-reflection."[48]

Such passages, indeed, would lead one to believe that, on the crucial question of the ego, Freud finally resorts to the teleological structure of analytic reflection for his model. But in fact this is not the case. On the contrary, the inviolable, irreducible core of Freud's primordial insight, and his faithfulness to it through all the transformations of psychoanalytic theory, shows itself with unparalleled clarity on this very point. The fact is that when Freud finally found it necessary to resurrect the ego, he fashioned his ego concept in terms of a primary narcissism such that the "great unity of the ego" is understood, not as the product of self-reflection, but as a compulsion to unity produced by the libidinal energies that reside in the ego. And primary narcissism has as its regulative idea, not the transparent self-consciousness of an ego identity, but the earliest configuration of psychical life imaginable—the "blissful isolation of intrauterine experience," which "on its psychical side" represents "the primal state of distribution of libido . . . total narcissism, in which the libido and ego-instincts, still united and indistinguishable, dwell in the self-sufficing ego."[49] Thus the unity of the ego in Freud's late theory is not modeled on the process of self-reflection. It originates in the unconscious self-absorption of the fetus, which precedes the irruption of the self into the world.

A Note on the Primacy of the Temporal Dimension

We have seen how, in seizing upon sexuality, with its resistance to complete reflective elucidation, as the guiding thread of analysis, and in taking the disclosure of the determinative fixations of an infantile prehistory as the basis for a recognition of the self within that analysis, Freud's intention was to read the evidences of reflection back to a ground in the densities of the body lived from within. A question arises here. How is it that temporality plays such a critical role in the grounding operation?

For Dilthey, recollection of the past simply elucidates the resolutely held consciousness of identity by retracing the course of development as something inwardly determined. Identity is a willfully constituted structure of moments that, through memory, recalls the process of its becoming. The temporality realized is by the same act annulled in the will-to-identity from which reflection departs and to which it returns. At bottom, the self for Dilthey is a synchronic entity. Not so for Freud's regressive movement into the past.

For psychoanalysis, temporality no longer has its source in a self recollecting its experience through time. Instead, the body itself grounds the experience of becoming. Reflection has access to the body *mediately* through the recollection of that experience along the path of the instincts. The reason Freud can conceive of the body as providing that ground is that evolutionary biology had already introduced temporality into the ground plan of nature as an essential element of organic being. On both the ontogenetic and phylogenetic levels, evolutionary biology envisions organic existence as a process in which complexity arises out of simplicity in a continuous sequence of temporally related developmental stages. Without at this point examining any further the significance of this matter from the side of biology, we simply note the words of a well-known contemporary mechanist biologist, François Jacob. "Living bodies," he writes, "are indissolubly bound up with time. In the living world, no structure can be detached from its history."[50] The animal essence of human existence already grounds our being in the single, unrepeatable sequence of birth, growth, decay, and death that circumscribes every life. In psychoanalysis, what is lived forward as body is realized backward as understanding. Dilthey's realization of temporality hinges on a virtual will-to-identity in which life, in the absence of any metaphysical meaning, falls back upon what is "known from within." Like Dilthey, Freud finds himself committed to the evidences of inwardness, to consciousness, as the basis for his science. He too is concerned with questions of meaning. But for Freud, life does point to something beyond whatever appears within it. It points to the inner, ultimately impenetrable darkness of the body. That is why the locus of meaning for Freud is not psychological but metapsychological. Metapsychology, we learned some time ago, initially meant biology, which Freud understood to be a reality behind and beyond but not discontinuous with psychology. Indeed, as he put it in 1913, psychoanalysis "acts as an intermediary between biology and psychology."[51]

Temporality is one of the keys to this intermediary role. Since temporality appears both as an objective property of biological being and as the subjective meaning realized in the recollection of experience, it provides the common ground that enables Freud to turn the body outside in within the framework of dualism. Temporality paved Freud's way between evolutionary biology and reflective philosophy. Through temporality, biology can have a meaning for human self-understanding. As we shall see, this matter is crucial to Freud's plotting of human reality on the cognitive map projected by the theory of evolution. But we must defer that matter until part II of this study. For we have yet to complete our consideration of the grounding operation.

CHAPTER 4

The Biological Ground

A final dimension of the grounding operation remains to be eluci-
dated. Our consideration of its two phases has brought us back to the
point where we began, to the metapsychological insight that transcends the fundamental disjunction of psychoanalytic discourse—to
the question, that is, of the instincts. For it is at the level of the instincts that the psychoanalytic perspective reaches the threshold between mind and body, between the *res cogitans* and the *res extensa*. "We regard instinct as being the concept on the frontier-line
between the somatic and the mental," Freud tells us in 1911 in
"Psycho-analytic Notes on an Autobiographical Account of a Case of
Paranoia *(Dementia Paranoides),*" known for short as the Schreber
case. Yet the instincts also mark the threshold that, in view of the
epistemological constraints under which it operates, psychoanalytic
theory cannot cross.[1]

In the initial unfolding of psychoanalytic theory, Freud does not
cross that threshold. In fact, before *Beyond the Pleasure Principle*
(1920) Freud had no instinct theory. But for one incidental reference, the very notion of a theory of the instincts does not appear in
Freud's writings until, in the Schreber case, Freud attests to the
need for "some well-grounded theory of the instincts; but in fact we
have nothing of the kind at our disposal."[2] Freud repeats this senti-
ment three years later in "On Narcissism: An Introduction" (1914),
where he complains of "the total absence of any theory of the instincts which would help us find our bearings."[3] Freud's words alert
us to the fact that by a theory of the instincts he means something
other than what he had accomplished in the *Three Essays*. But if, in

its initial unfolding, psychoanalytic theory has no theory of the instincts, what is it that guides the movements of the grounding operation?

According to the epistemological clarifications found in the introduction to the 1915 edition, the *Three Essays* constitutes an investigation "made possible through the technique of psycho-analysis," whose "aim has . . . been to discover how far psychological investigations can throw light upon the biology of the sexual life of man."[4] Rather than developing its own theory of the instincts, the *Three Essays* stands within one taken ready-made from biology. In laying out the groundwork of psychoanalytic understanding, Freud turned to the authoritative science of organic phenomena and underwrote the grounding operation with the rudimentary biological distinction between the functions of reproduction and self-production, whose correlative instincts are sexuality and self-preservation. In conformity with the occlusion of the ego that characterizes the grounding operation, Freud brackets the self-preservative instinct and devotes himself in the *Three Essays* exclusively to the psychoanalytic investigation of the sexual instinct.

Freud makes the biological provenance of this theoretical underpinning explicit in "On Narcissism"—in the period, that is, when he introduces the notion of a theory of the instincts in order to denote a lacuna in psychoanalytic theory.

> I try in general to keep psychology clear from everything that is different in nature from it, *even biological lines of thought.* For that very reason I should like at this point expressly to admit that the hypothesis of separate ego-instincts and sexual instincts (that is to say, libido theory) *rests scarcely at all upon a psychological basis, but derives its principal support from biology.* [my italics][5]

In 1931 he offered a revealing *apologia* for this procedure. "Of all the slowly developed parts of analytic theory, the theory of the instincts is the one that has felt its way the most painfully forward. And yet the theory was so indispensable to the whole structure that something had to be put in its place."[6] In light of what we have shown to be the relationship of psychoanalytic thought to Darwinian theory, it should be no mystery why Freud considered the theory of the instincts indispensable. A question arises here, however. How, in lieu of a theory of the instincts, was the biological hypothesis able to support Freud's original theoretical structure? In answering this question, we shall bring the elucidation of the grounding operation to a close.

The Place of the Biological Hypothesis

Freud's reliance on the authority of biological science originally served psychoanalytic theory as an important source of support, even though that support came from a science whose field of phenomena was external to that which Freud had resolved to confine himself to. If psychoanalytic investigation of man's inwardness could be shown to coincide with what was known about organic phenomena as data within the realm of the extended and material, then the psychoanalytic claim to be a science of the mind would be greatly enhanced. "After we have completed our psycho-analytic work we shall have to find a point of contact with biology; and we may rightfully feel glad if that contact is already secured at one important point or another."[7] In positing the body as the ground to be approached but never grasped from within, Freud exhibits a scrupulous respect for the constraints of dualism. What is crucial to remember here is that what commanded respect for those constraints was science itself. For Descartes's distinction between the *res cogitans* and the *res extensa* has maintained its powerful grip over the modern mind not by virtue of its philosophical cogency. On the contrary, dualism has represented a conundrum for philosophy and common sense alike. The mind–body problem has been for the modern age what Zeno's paradoxes were for antiquity. What has caused modern man to run up against this problem time and again is the weighty catalog of natural science's practically efficacious cognitive achievements—achievements which, as long as they were taken to embody truthful disclosures of the hidden mechanisms of nature, demanded the excision of everything associated with mentation from the domain of nature's objectivity. This excision is exactly what Cartesianism realized.

As we have seen, however, Darwin's closing of the circle of science by enfolding within nature a being that is mindful of its existence deprives dualism of its raison d'être. This is where our interpretation of Freud got its footing by demonstrating how psychoanalysis responds to this new situation of understanding. Bound by the very accomplishments of Darwin to the authority of science, and thereby to the dualistic ontology it projects, Freud responds to this novel situation with an equally novel manipulation of what is already "known" from the standpoint of science's self-certainty in its knowledge of nature. Thus in the last synoptic presentation of his thought, "An Outline of Psycho-analysis" (1940), Freud articulates what he calls the "basic assumption" of psychoanalysis: "We know two kinds of things about what we call our psyche (or mental life): First its bodily organ and scene of action, the brain (or nervous system), and, on the other hand, our acts of consciousness which are immediate data and cannot be further explained by any sort of description."[8] "Brain (or nervous system)" and "acts of consciousness" are not presented here as empirical data delimited by theoretical constructs, though at bottom that is what they are. Instead, they represent the two "kinds of things" that are known about our mental life before any investigation of it begins.

These two kinds of things are already known beforehand because even where acts of consciousness are treated as an epiphenomenal residue that "haunts" the material processes of the brain, science certifies both of these knowns as the self-evident dual manifestations of the selfsame reality. As self-evident knowns, they are the two antithetical but equally certain kinds of phenomena that assure us a secure epistemic grip on the reality called mental life. It is here that biological science—a science of material reality—initially provides psychoanalysis an invaluable service by supplying Freud with the rudimentary articulation of the functions of organism as *objective* data whose reality becomes manifest *subjectively* as mind along the neuronal pathways that reach the brain and in the brain itself. Indeed, since the inward "known" of mental life delimits the field of phenomena Freud chose to cultivate, he had literally nowhere else to turn but to the biological sciences to gain his bearings toward the material side of mental life that, by definition, lay beyond the reach of psychoanalytic investigation. For although the technique of free association, starting with the inward "known," enables Freud to unmask the dissimulations of desire that pervade consciousness and to penetrate the depths of the unconscious, the path into those depths required metapsychological guidance if it was to stay oriented toward the other "known" and not lose its way in the darkness of the unconscious. For Freud, that darkness signified the body itself.

The fact that the unconscious is "in itself" unknowable coincides perfectly with the fact that the body's "known" manifestation is itself external. As the scientifically certified articulation of the body, the biological hypothesis assures Freud's grip on what is externally known. By grasping from without what is to be approached from within, psychoanalytic theory secures a metapsychological guide as well as the assurance of the scientific integrity of its endeavor. Thus, in grasping sexuality as the ground of the mind's inner being, Freud manages to manipulate Descartes's ontological dualism into a framework of understanding that surmounts dualism—that transforms its antithetical domains into a continuum without violating its epistemological constraints. "Let us grant to nature," he wrote Groddeck in 1917, "her infinite variety, which rises from the inanimate to the organically animated, from the just physically alive to the spiritual. No doubt the Ucs. is the right mediator between the mental and the physical, perhaps it is the long-sought-for 'missing link.' "[9] In the dark realm of the unconscious inserted *between* mind and body, Freud thought he had discovered the epistemic space for the investigation of the mind's bodily ground.

These considerations serve to explain in principle how the biological hypothesis could be used to underwrite the grounding operation. But two further things need to be explained. First, what justified Freud's bracketing of the self-preservative instincts and focus on the biological function of sexuality? Second, how is Freud able to identify the mental manifestations of sexuality with the apparently nonsexual manifestations of dreams and neurotic symptoms? The answer to the second question follows from the answer to the first. And here the argumentation of the *Three Essays* is subordinate to considerations of a different sort. For our first question does not direct us to the issue of how the psychoanalytic investigation of sexuality is carried out, or to the theoretical equations by which the results of that investigation are coordinated with the psychology of the unconscious articulated in *The Interpretation of Dreams*. As we shall see, these matters are transparent enough. What is not transparent, but must largely be inferred, is the *biological* reasoning that brought Freud to fix so adamantly on *sexuality* as the elementary instinctual force whose vicissitudes and transformations give rise to the manifestations of meaning that structure unconscious mental life. Thus our excavation of psychoanalytic theory must penetrate beneath the foundations of Freud's theoretical structure into the biological bedrock in which those foundations are planted.

The Utilization of the Biological Hypothesis

For Freud, mind has no meaning beyond its natural history in the living of life. An instinct is not a stable "something" but an activity that persists through time. "An instinct . . . never operates as a force giving a *momentary* impact but always as a *constant* one. . . . The characteristic of exercising pressure is common to all instincts; it is in fact their very essence. Every instinct is a piece of activity."[10] With Dilthey, Freud might have said, "When the self penetrates earnestly into itself, it finds itself not as substance, being, fact, but as life, activity, energy."[11] But psychoanalysis is not a pure phenomenology of the life process. Life, activity, and energy, if they are to become determinate objectifications of scientific cognition, must be referred to the biological functions of the human organism. To this end the *Three Essays* embarks on a psychoanalytic investigation of territory marked out for it beforehand by biology. Hence the opening lines of the *Three Essays:*

> The fact of the existence of sexual needs in human beings and animals is expressed in biology by the assumption of a 'sexual instinct', on the analogy of the instinct of nutrition, that is hunger. Everyday language possesses no counterpart to the word 'hunger', but science makes use of the word 'libido' for that purpose.[12]

Our task is to explain with what justification Freud fixed on the biological function of sexuality, and not, for instance, of nutrition, as the inward ground of the appearances of mind.

What enables the sexual function to define and delimit the material basis of psychical reality is the unique position biological science accords to sexuality in the processes of organic existence. Freud himself articulates this matter in the passage in "On Narcissism" where he examines the reasons for his previously tacit adoption of the biological hypothesis. His terms of reference are those of August Weismann, whose genetic theories were instrumental in repelling Lamarckian and vitalist assaults on Darwin's evolutionary mechanics at the end of the last century, and in thus opening the way to the contemporary synthesis of genetics and Darwinism that is the prevailing orthodoxy.

In "On Narcissism" Freud appeals to Weismann's morphological distinction between soma and germ cells as the basis for his adoption of the biological hypothesis of separate sexual and self-preservative (ego) instincts.[13]

> The individual does actually carry on a twofold existence: one to serve his own purposes and the other as a link in a chain, which he serves against his will, or at least involuntarily. The individual himself regards sexuality as one of his own ends; whereas from another point of view he is an appendage to his germ-plasm, at whose disposal he puts his energies in return for a bonus of pleasure. He is the mortal vehicle of a (possibly) immortal substance—like the inheritor of an entailed property, who is only the temporary holder of an estate which survives him. The separation of the sexual instincts from the ego-instincts would simply reflect this twofold function of the individual.[14]

What was it about the unique role of sexuality in defining the twofold existence of the individual that enabled it to serve the needs of psychoanalytic theory? What was crucial, I suspect, was the *distinction* between self-preservation and reproduction read as instinctual activities. The "sexual function," as Freud puts it in the *Introductory Lectures*, "is the single function of a living organism which extends beyond the individual and is concerned with his relation to the species. It is an unmistakeable fact that it does not always, like the individual organism's other functions, bring it advantages, but, in return for an unusually high degree of pleasure, brings dangers which threaten the individual's life and often enough destroy it."[15] Thus, from a biological standpoint, sexuality represents a force that operates independently of those activities of the organism directed at maintaining its life. This unique position of sexuality is reflected in the argument of the *Origin of Species* where Darwin speaks of the mechanism of "sexual selection." Sexual selection "depends not on a struggle for existence, but on a struggle between males for the possession of females"[16]—which, incidentally, is the hypothesis Freud adopts in *Totem and Taboo* for the famous story of the "primal crime." Let us consider further, however, the distinctive position of sexuality in the functioning of the individual organism by considering it in relation to adaptation—the concept that is to Darwin's theory of evolution what force is to Newton's rational mechanics. It is by going in this direction that we shall learn why Freud fixed on sexuality.

Adaptation pertains to the relationship of the organism and its environment. Adaptation means fitness to the environment and has no meaning outside the context of organism and environment viewed in conjunction. In the context of natural selection, adaptation is, strictly speaking, a nonfalsifiable concept. Death is the price of nonadaptation, thus quickly eliminating the presence of counterexamples.[17] This stark alternative of life or death, being or nonbeing, is what imparts to the mechanics of evolution its element of causal necessity.

Despite the substantive indeterminacy of the concept of adaptation—for virtually any corporeal or behavioral structure counts as adaptive so long as it works—the idea of fitness indicates its operative sense. Since every organism's means to life are external to it, its transactions with the environment are obligatory. To keep itself in being, an organism must be fit for the external conditions upon which it depends to sustain its metabolic processes. Adaptation thus directs us to the transactional intermeshings of the organism and its environment—intermeshings whose shameless utilitarianism is governed by organic necessity. Viewed globally, the kingdom of life thus constitutes what Darwin called an "economy of nature" characterized by the "infinitely complex and close-fitting material relations of all organic beings to each other and to their physical conditions of life."[18]

The sexual activities of the organism also participate in this economy of nature and must also be adapted to the organic and inorganic conditions of life if they are to fulfill their function of securing the reproduction of the species. However, in the case of sexuality the law of biological necessity—adapt or perish—pertains not to the individual organism but to the species itself. This fact marks out sexuality as a function that is superfluous to the survival of the individual organism. In Darwin's words, the "result of sexual selection is not death to the unsuccessful competitor, but fewer or no offspring. Sexual selection is, therefore, less rigorous than natural selection."[19] Sexual selection is less rigorous than natural selection because the sexual function is not bound to the urgent imperatives of survival governing the strictly utilitarian activities of self-perservation. The sexual instincts, therefore, denote a source of potential surplus en-

ergy capable of manifesting itself in nonadaptive, nonfunctional
forms.

In the *Three Essays* Freud exploits this potentiality for nonadaptive manifestation by beginning his psychoanalytic investigation of
sexuality with what, from the standpoint of the biological function of
sexuality, are patently nonfunctional but indubitably sexual activity—namely, the perversions. As the realization of the sexual instinct's potentiality for nonadaptive manifestation, the perversions
play a twofold role in the psychoanalytic investigation of sexuality.
First, they accord an emphatically sexual significance to those organs—primarily eyes, mouth, and anus—which, while implicated in
the act of "normal," that is, biologically functional sexuality, nonetheless are not, anatomically speaking, part of the body's sexual
equipment. From the perspective of the standpoint of psychoanalysis on the side of the body lived from within, the perversions thus
attest to a dimension of "organ-pleasure"—of the organism's enjoy-
ment of its own bodily activities—that eludes the vision of a biological science which is fixed on the organism's environmentally directed "utility-functioning." From the experientially determinate
configurations of organ-pleasure afforded by the perversions, Freud
derives his famous inference of an autoerotic, polymorphous, perverse infantile sexuality. What is critical here is that Freud's argument gains its ground of possibility from the strictly *biological* fact
of sexuality's freedom from the iron law of necessity governing the
survival activities of the organism.

In the capacity for nonadaptive, nonfunctional manifestation realized positively by the perversions, sexuality becomes available as
a biologically based energic potential that can also be called upon to
account for those apparently nonerotic aspects of human reality that
transcend the utilitarian preoccupations of physical survival. This is
the second function the perversions play in the *Three Essays*. Here
the nonadaptive behavior of the neurotic, whose "mental break-
down" marks a withdrawal from the business of everyday life, is
what pointed Freud to the work of sexual energy as its biological
ground of possibility. In order to derive the compulsiveness of the
neurotic from the reservoir of sexual surplus energy, Freud postulated a diversion of libido from patently sexual employments to
other activities. This notion of diversion is secured and elaborated

first in the psychology of the unconscious by the mechanism of repression and by the postulation of the primary processes of displacement and condensation as governing the domain of unconscious meaning. Correlatively, the theory of psychosexual development laid out in the *Three Essays* postulates a latency period during which reaction-formations and sublimations arise to divert and transform the flow of libido, thereby bringing the children of nature under the sway of civil society. I shall not detail here all the complexities and difficulties this theory embroils Freud in. The point I wish to make is simply this: since, by definition, the energies of self-preservation are absorbed in the obligatory transactions of the organism with its environment, the potentiality of sexuality to abstain from intercourse with the external world is exactly what accords it the "power to shape our inner life-history," as Binswanger once put it.[20] Moreover, the very necessity governing the utilitarian transactions of self-preservation signifies that external reality is the ultimate source of the frustration of libido—a frustration of impulse that generates the inner life history as a depth networked by the dissimulations and distortions of unrealized desire. Frustration by the necessity that governs the external world is what transforms somatic impulses into unfulfilled wishes that continue to press for satisfaction. Between the unknowable ground of the unconscious and the manifestations of mind appearing on the surface of consciousness lies the network of meanings that it is the task of interpretation to uncover. Dreams and neurotic symptoms, which attest to inner depths that stand in opposition to the necessities of external reality, can then be read as the transformations of libido. The link between unconscious meaning and sexual energy is forged in the *Three Essays* by equating them in an inverse relationship. Neurotic symptoms are there defined as "the sexual activity of the patient."[21] "They are formed in part at the cost of *abnormal* sexuality; *neuroses are, so to say, the negative of perversions.*"[22]

To summarize the point of these considerations: what justified Freud's fixation on sexuality as the basis of man's inner life history was not his patients' persistent references to their sex lives but the biological *distinction* between self-preservation and sexuality—a distinction which assured him that only sexuality could afford the luxury of undergoing the transformations requisite to the multi-valences of meaning disclosed by the work of interpretation. Once again, Freud's theoretical vision framed the ultimate meaning of his practical findings.

We have seen, then, how the biological hypothesis was able to underwrite the grounding operation, how the sexual instincts, in distinction from the self-preservative ego instincts, afforded Freud a justification for attributing an instinctual basis to the otherwise preternatural inner life-world of the mind. By planting himself upon somatic territory whose rudimentary dimensions were already marked out by biological science, and by bracketing the ego and exploiting the biological ground of possibility offered by sexuality, Freud placed the foundations of the psychoanalytic theory on eminently respectable and defensible epistemological grounds. By adhering to the authority of biological science and grasping from without what psychoanalysis, in scrupulous regard for the constraints of dualism, could approach only from within, Freud turned his epistemological limitations into a source of strength. Freud had found in biology a beacon to light the darkness within.

PART II

PSYCHOANALYSIS, EVOLUTION, AND THE END OF METAPHYSICS

Metaphysics actually exists, if not as
a science, yet still as natural disposition
(metaphysica naturalis). For human reason,
without being moved merely by idle desire for
extent and variety of knowledge, proceeds
impetuously, driven on by an inward need
to questions such as cannot be answered
by any empirical employment of reason, or
by principles thence derived. Thus in all
men, as soon as their reason has become
ripe for speculation, there has always
existed and will always continue to exist
some kind of metaphysics.

—Immanuel Kant, 1787

Other defects in my nature have certainly
distressed me and made me feel humble;
with metaphysics it is different—I not
only have no talent for it, but no respect
for it either. In secret—one cannot say
such things aloud—I believe that one day
metaphysics will be condemned as a nuisance,
an abuse of thinking, a survival from the
period of the religious *Weltanschauung*.
I know to what extent this estranges me
from German cultural life.

—Sigmund Freud, 1927

We found that an inner tension propels the movement of psychoanalytic theory. That tension arises from the circumstance that Freud posits the body within the mind as the ground to be approached through reflection, while at the same time he adheres to the onto-epistemological discipline of dualism—a discipline that would seem from the outset to preclude just such a relationship. We thematized that tension and called it Freud's ground problem. And we tried to show that the attempt to secure an organic ground for the domain of psychical phenomena was not a fortuitous intellectual happening, but was conditioned and prompted by the problematic situation of understanding Darwin created by achieving an explanation for the origins and development of living entities that satisfied the epistemic requirements of natural science. Let us recall the logic of this relationship between Darwin and Freud.

From the standpoint of reflection, one immediate consequence of Darwin's achievement—though this is not necessarily how contemporaries formulated the matter—is the enfolding of mind within the nature it seeks to understand. With this, the existential status of man, as that status had been secured by the self-positing reason of the thinking ego in the tradition of reflective thought, becomes equivocal. On the one hand, the psychical phenomena that come into view in the act of reflection cannot be assigned a place on the side of the *res extensa*, whose ontological dignity depends, after all, on the exclusion of those very phenomena. On the other hand, psychical phenomena can no longer take up a place in the hierarchy established by the self-explication of the reflecting ego, for with evolution the mind has literally thought that ground out from beneath itself. By placing organic being before the understanding as the ultimate referent for all the evidences of human existence, Darwinism itself suggests an alternative—an alternative obviated by the heritage of dualism, with its irresoluble disjunction between mind and body, but one that has been advanced emphatically by the various schools of reflective biology that have arisen as the unorthodox complement to Darwinism.[1] That alternative, to which Darwinism by virtue of its irrevocable methodological commitments remains blind, is the tracing of the evidences of mind back to a ground in the body lived from within.[2]

In trying to reach that alternative ground, Freud operates within the framework of dualism rather than transcending it. After his crude attempt to seize hold directly of "physical reality" by reading the activity of neurons in the manifestations of consciousness, Freud resolved to confine himself to the field of psychical phenomena as the irreducible material of his theoretical and empirical elaborations. But this resolve did not mean that he abandoned his biological convictions. "I . . . have no desire at all," he wrote Fleiss in 1898, "to leave the psychology hanging in the air with no organic basis. But beyond the feeling of conviction [that there must be such a basis], I have nothing, either theoretical or therapeutic, to work on, and so I must behave as if I were confronted by psychological factors only. I have no idea why I cannot yet fit it together."[3] Six months earlier, however, Freud had had a momentary vision of how to fit it together—a vision whose essence he captured with the term *metapsychology*. Metapsychology, as the term is situated in this initial usage, means biology—a reality that stands both behind and beyond the sphere of the psychical while remaining nonetheless approachable through that sphere. It is in the context of metapsychology so understood that Freud announces his intention to take the body lived from within as his ground.

That intention is carried out in the founding works of psychoanalysis by a diphasic grounding operation. Reduced to their most elementary terms, those two phases consist, first, in the determination that unconscious wishful impulses lie at the root of mental life and, second, in the further resolution of those impulses into experientially fixed, somatogenic sources of libidinal energy. To underwrite this enterprise, Freud draws on the accumulated capital of biological science. By deploying the biological distinction between the sexual and self-preservative instincts, Freud is able to secure a ground in organic reality without violating the constraints of dualism. The biological hypothesis thus enables him to keep the theory of the instincts off his agenda, while at the same time establishing a crucial point of contact with the science of life.

The psychoanalytic venture does not end with *The Interpretation of Dreams* and the *Three Essays on the Theory of Sexuality*. On the contrary, Freud reaches an unanticipated turning point when, beginning in the summer of 1910, he undertakes the project that came to be *Totem and Taboo* (1912–13). *Totem and Taboo* initiates a cycle of developments that results in the virtual metamorphosis of psychoanalytic theory. The cycle begins when, in preparation for addressing the question of cultural phenomena in *Totem and Taboo,* Freud makes an extension of libido theory by introducing the concept of narcissism. In this, Freud preserves an essential point of continuity with his original psychology. But the outcome of the cycle is a theoretical structure radically disjunctive with the original. What the biological hypothesis had enabled Freud to keep off the agenda of psychoanalytic theory now appears at its core. In the place of the biological hypothesis stands the theory of the Eros and death instincts. At the same time, the ego, which Freud had hoped he could dispense with, returns. More correctly, the ego is resurrected, for the grounding operation had, so to speak, marked its crucifixion.

Despite the disjunctions between Freud's early and late theories, psychoanalysis constitutes a single-minded, continuous course of development—a theoretical venture governed by a resolute adherence to its original insights and aims. The subsequent episodes of this study are devoted to showing how this is so.

As he turned, in December of 1911, to devote his theoretical energies exclusively to *Totem and Taboo,* Freud reached a moment of reckoning. His work, he complained to Jung, still at that point a close collaborator and confidant, was not going well.

> I have very little time and to draw on books and reports is not at all the same as drawing on the richness of one's own experience. Besides, my interest is diminished by the conviction that I am already in possession of the truths I am trying to prove. Such truths, of course, are of no use to anyone else. I can see from the difficulties I encounter in this work that I was not cut out for inductive investigation, that my whole make-up is intuitive, and that in setting out to establish the purely empirical science of ψα [psychoanalysis] I subjected myself to an extraordinary discipline.[4]

What Freud came to see in this moment of reckoning is that he had subjected himself to the extraordinary discipline of science for reasons that were themselves extrascientific—that his deepest insights were not scientific cognitions at all but recognitions of meaning, intuitions of truth. In fact, as we shall see, Freud's odyssey of understanding was governed from beginning to end by a fundamentally philosophical insight—an insight that by its very nature forced Freud to submit to the cognitive discipline of science. The hidden theme of psychoanalytic theory is the end of metaphysics; its hidden aim, to bring the tradition of Western metaphysics to a definitive close on behalf of natural science, to exorcise once and for all the metaphysical specter which, even in an age enlightened by science, has haunted the Western outlook.

CHAPTER 5

Desire as the Human Essence

The key to Freud's vision and to the place of his thought within Western speculation about man can be stated simply: psychoanalysis realizes the end of metaphysics by elaborating the meaning of Darwinism for human self-understanding. By this I do not mean that Freud had such a project in mind as a formal program of thought. Rather, evolution was for Freud an indubitable reality. Psychoanalytic theory arose out of the genuine perplexities surrounding the question of man in light of the reality Darwin had disclosed. Still, psychoanalysis is no evolutionary anthropology, at least not in any conventional sense, for Freud does not approach the phenomenon of man from the methodological perspective of evolutionary biology. That is, he does not reflect on human evidences with a view to discovering the relative survival advantages, and thus the raison d'être, of such distinctive features of *homo sapiens* as language, tool fabrication and use, or the upright posture. Instead of the biological meaning of being human, psychoanalysis is concerned with the human meaning of being a biological entity, and with finding a way of making that meaning the basis of our self-understanding, both as individuals and as species members. It is the question of meaning that sustains the speculative vitality of psychoanalytic theory and forms its point of critical engagement with the metaphysical tradition.

A single, primordial insight initiates the psychoanalytic venture and remains its pole of orientation throughout. That single insight constitutes a redefinition of the human essence. With Darwin, science brought into its view a nature with man in it. Freud realizes the meaning of this discovery by redefining the human essence as *de-*

sire—as the welling up of the body from within. The decisive formulations for the determination of that essence are found in *The
Interpretation of Dreams*.

The Interpretation of Dreams shares with Heidegger's *Being
and Time* (1927) the sensibility that the overwhelming reality of
everyday life closes the individual off from a confrontation with the
authentic self.[1] For the pursuit of that self, Freud bids us turn to our
dreams with a mind to discovering its hidden meaning there. While
thus elevating the dream and making it the manifestation of the
mind's authentic originality, *The Interpretation of Dreams* at the
same time divests of substance the mind's emphatic expression as
self-conscious reason and substantializes in its stead an unconscious
domain of sheer impulse. For that domain, suppressed in waking
life, is what gains expression (albeit a distorted one requiring interpretation) in dreams. With the withdrawal of external reality in
sleep, there is "an alteration in the play of forces between the powers of mental life."[2] Dreams are what the mind produces wholly out
of itself when freed from the need to attend to the distractions that
intrude upon it from without.

"Man is explicitly man," Hegel informs us in the preface to the
Phenomenology of Mind, "only in the form of developed and cul-
tivated reason, which has made itself to be what it is implicitly."[3]
Against this identification of the human essence with reason's reflective self-explication must be placed Freud's assertion, at the end
of the dream book, that the "core of our being" consists "of unconscious wishful impulses."[4] Between the two formulations stands
Darwin, who brings the Copernican-Galilean revolution—which
had extruded man from nature—around full circle to embrace man
himself. The result is that the subordination of life to the discipline
of reason, which forms an essential aspect of both ancient and modern metaphysics, is inverted by psychoanalysis into a subordination
of reason to the vicissitudes of life. For Hegel, metaphysics begins
in the naive self-consciousness of the individual who realizes himself to be "the immediate certainty of self . . . unconditioned
being."[5] Similarly, Freud's psychoanalysis takes "acts of consciousness" to be "immediate data" that are "without parallel" and that
"defy all explanation or description."[6] The immediate self-certainty
of consciousness with which both men begin, however, also marks
the point of departure for two radically different ventures. In con-

trast to Hegel's *Phenomenology*, psychoanalytic reflection stands in the shadow of Darwin, of the knowledge ascertained by the science of external reality that "we human beings are rooted in our animal nature."[7] Without abandoning the field of phenomena first delimited by reflective philosophy, Freud makes recourse to natural history for the determination of the human essence, and this in the first instance means recourse to dreams for the determination of the hidden turnings of desire of which the authentic self consists. For the natural history of the mind lies in these hidden turnings, which the science of the unconscious is charged with disclosing.

In the founding works of psychoanalysis, Freud's aims are limited. He is not yet aware of just how radical the implications of his definitive insight are. Thus his assertion that not reason but unconscious wishful impulses form the core of our being does not prevent him from fixing the relations of reason and impulse in the traditional hierarchy of higher and lower human faculties. In full accord with that traditional hierarchy, the aim of psychoanalysis, according to the dream book, is to bring heteronomous unconscious impulses "under the domination of" rational psychical processes, as is the case for normal mental functioning.[8] Unconscious wishful impulses cannot be the essence of man, as I have claimed to be the case for psychoanalysis, if some higher power controls them.

Freud's choice of the word domination is telling here, and enables us to resolve this apparent contradiction. In Freud, reason becomes an instrument of psychical domination rather than the realization of a rationally determined harmony of the soul because it has lost its metaphysical sanction. To put the matter another way, lacking metaphysical justification, reason loses all substantive content, all norm-giving force, and becomes merely a necessity-imposed regulative function of the "mental apparatus"—a means among means in the technique of living that is unable itself to determine the sense of living. Organic need is what sustains that sense for Freud. The activity of reflection in the work of dream interpretation is not the explication by reason of what it is implicitly but the clearing away of the "obscurity in which the center of our being . . . is veiled from our knowledge."[9]

We must pause here, however, to address a stronger objection to the whole line of argument we are developing—the objection that our argument is based upon a fundamental misreading of the dream book. *The Interpretation of Dreams*, it can be countered, in no way sets out to demonstrate a pre-given concept of the human essence based upon some insight into the implications of Darwinism for the concept of man. Rather, *The Interpretation of Dreams* gains all its insights from the work of interpreting the meaning of dreams. What Freud then does with the results of dream interpretation, in terms either of deriving from those results some general propositions concerning human nature, or of coordinating the psychological motives dream interpretation discloses with instinctual drives arising from the unconscious, is a separate matter that has no bearing on the findings of the work of interpretation itself. As Paul Ricoeur puts it, the "vicissitudes of the instincts . . . can be attained only in the vicissitudes of meaning,"[10] and not the other way around. That unconscious wishful impulses form the core of our being only summarizes what interpretation has disclosed. Fundamentally, *The Interpretation of Dreams* develops a form of language analysis whose concern is to determine reflectively the meaning of the discrete empirical products of the sleeping mind, and not to give concrete determination to some abstractly conceived, global definition of the human essence.

This portrayal of *The Interpretation of Dreams* is not entirely wrong. But in turning us to the work of interpretation as the essential basis of psychoanalytic insight, it fails to come to grips with some fundamental aspects of Freud's theory of dreams that indicate otherwise.

First of all, as a "psychical structure with a meaning,"[11] the dream presents us, Freud argues, with a fundamentally imagistic, prelinguistic mode of expression. Dreams, that is, differ radically from waking thought processes in that they think predominantly in images and not concepts, and replace thoughts with hallucinations. With certain exceptions, which Freud tries to argue away, the dream is thus not a linguistic text but a pictographic one. Second, dreams do not express meaning in all its possibilities but only a particular modality of meaning. Dreams are uniformly (hallucinatory) fulfillments of wishes, and thus the dream becomes the basis for subordinating all meaning to the monolithism of the wish. The case Freud finally makes for the wish-fulfillment thesis is one that transcends all interpretative, empirical considerations. "Thought is after all nothing but a substitute for a hallucinatory wish," he announces categorically in chapter 7, "and it is self-evident that dreams must be wish fulfilments, since nothing but a wish can set our mental apparatus at work."[12] The imagistic nature of oneiric phenomena and the wish-fulfilling nature of oneiric meaning are brought together and given a common source by Freud in what he calls the "experience of satisfaction."[13] The experience of satisfaction is a function of being organic and constitutes the original datum of human life as lived—a datum from which all meaning, whatever its latter vicissitudes, arises.

However suggestive, none of this is decisive for undercutting the argument for the primacy of interpretation in Freud's theory of dreams. What is decisive is the fact that the method for disclosing meaning—the technique of interpretation—is itself designed to elicit the modality of meaning dreams are said to express. Free association—the technique Freud developed after the *Studies on Hysteria* and in conjunction with the formulation of the dream book—requires that two changes be brought about in the mental attitude of the person engaging in it, "an increase in the attention he pays to his own psychical perceptions and the elimination of the criticism by which he normally sifts the thoughts that occur to him."[14] In the state of free-associative self-observation, the subject abstains from reflectively working over his thoughts and instead adopts the stance of a neutral observer whose efforts are concentrated on reporting faithfully whatever happens to pass through his mind.

The adoption of this technique for deciphering dream phenomena already leads Freud to eliminate certain elements of the manifest dream as material unfit for interpretation. Ironically, those are the elements of apparent intelligibility, of which the most important is the aspect of overall coherence many dreams have. Freud attributes this coherence to a "secondary revision" and compares it to the facade of an Italian church—to an outward show of order that bears no relation to the structure lying behind it.

Our concern, however, is not with such subtleties of Freud's theory of dreams, revealing though they may be. Instead, a much more obvious feature of Freud's technique of interpretation presents itself for consideration. For as long as the critical, deliberative activity of reflection, which Freud contrasts explicitly with the process of free association,[15] is in abeyance, what other logic does the mind have to

guide it but the logic of impulse, desire, affect, feeling? Is it any sur-
prise that the application of free association to a dream will always
reveal a network of hidden desires connected with it?

The categorical assertion that, since only a wish can set our mental
apparatus at work, dreams are self-evidently wish fulfillments Freud
saves for the seventh and last chapter of the dream book, whose argument is epistemologically disjunctive with the earlier chapters. In
the first six chapters Freud tries to make his case by staying entirely
within the limits of the work of interpretation and what can be inferred from it. But on the crucial matter of the wish-fulfillment thesis, the most he can assert within those limits is, "the fact that dreams
really have a secret meaning which represents the fulfilment of a
wish must be proved afresh in each particular case by analysis."[16]
This he can safely assert since, so long as the technique of interpretation is employed properly, it will always discover that concealed
behind the manifest content of the dream lie wishes striving for
expression.

The characterization I have given to Freud's interpretative technique does not constitute an argument against the validity of the results obtained by dream interpretation, or of the theory concerning
the nature of dreams confirmed by those results. On the contrary, no
method can be expected to be efficacious unless it is somehow at-
tuned to the reality of the phenomenon it seeks to understand or explain. In any case, the question of validity itself is not what concerns
me here. All I mean to argue is that, questions of validity aside, the
technique of interpretation is itself based on a prior understanding
of the nature of dreams. To put it the other way around, the wish-
fulfilling nature of oneiric meaning is not something arrived at in-
ductively from the results of interpretation. Rather, it informs, and
probably even guided, Freud to the development of the technique
which discloses that meaning concretely in each case. The insight
that wishful impulses constitute the core of our being precedes the
work of interpretation that demonstrates it. Dream interpretation is
a way of focusing the light of consciousness upon that core and, by a
process of inference, of conceptually fixing the dream as the text of
the authentic self.

In none of this do I argue that explicitly biological considerations
enter into the formulations of the core argument of the dream book,
which are delimited by the work of interpretation. The same cannot

be said, however, for chapter 7, where the "experience of satisfaction" is critical to the assimilation of the dream into a general psychology. Indeed, in the crucial transitional passages introducing that chapter, Freud remarks, "It is only after we have disposed of everything having to do with the work of interpretation that we can begin to realize the incompleteness of our psychology of dreams."[17] What I am saying is that even where the work of interpretation is central to its argument, *The Interpretation of Dreams* is based on an insight into what the essence of man must be in the light of what Darwin taught. For reasons we shall come later to appreciate, the 'wish' is the perfect choice for the expression of that essence. *The Interpretation of Dreams* shows men how, by turning away from the externally imposed positivities of waking life, they can gain access to what lies at the core of their being and consolidate a self-understanding within its terms of reference.

CHAPTER 6

The End of Metaphysics

Freud's Disavowal of Metaphysics

The old-fashioned phrase "essence of man" has appeared several times in the course of this discussion, and this is the point to explain why. The reasons have to do with the internal relationship that Freud's thought establishes between itself and metaphysics. The psychoanalytic perspective articulated by Freud entails a disavowal of metaphysics. But this disavowal is not that of a positivist oblivious to the concerns that animated metaphysical speculation. Nor is it an incidental consequence of the psychoanalytic outlook. Rather, psychoanalytic thought is fundamentally oriented by that disavowal, and bears within itself the mark of metaphysics by virtue of that disavowal. That mark is the essentialism that sustains the psychoanalytic vision of human reality. Essentialism, the notion that a single principle or substance underlies all the manifestations of a particular entity, thereby making it be what it is, has its provenance in the heritage of metaphysics—a heritage which, cast adrift from its moorings by the Copernican revolution, suffered shipwreck in the nineteenth century. That unconscious wishful impulses constitute the core of our being is the definitive insight around which Freud's theory of man crystallizes. As a consequence, Freud's thought perpetuates essentialism in the aftermath of metaphysics by realizing the sense of essentialism in a radically altered setting. Evolutionism established that new setting by being the instrument through which natural science could finally make a serious claim upon the totality of the existent. Psychoanalysis allies itself with this claim and tries to make it good by reading man back into nature without prejudice to the innermost, intimate evidences of the human presence within the existent.

To articulate this matter in terms of a perpetuation of essentialism without the support of metaphysics would seem to involve a fundamental contradiction. For the fact of the matter is that the implicit ontology of natural science—perhaps best expressed in the notion of reality as process—is profoundly antiessentialist. Darwin's "completion of the Copernican revolution in ontology" (Jonas) consists precisely in the dissolution of essentialism's last stronghold—namely, living nature, whose organisms, both individually and in their mutual interrelations, seem to manifest some kind of teleological order. Despite its elimination of purpose from the kingdom of life, however, Darwinism itself provided the setting for Freud's reconstitution of human being in accordance with a perception of its essence. But before we can explain how this is so, we must first demonstrate what we have thus far only asserted—namely, that Freud's turn to natural history draws its strength and its rudimentary orientation from his turn away from metaphysics.

"The intellectual period . . . has now been left behind," we are told in the early pages of *The Interpretation of Dreams*, "when the human mind was dominated by philosophy and not by the exact natural sciences."[1] Yet that realization did not deter Freud, in private correspondence, from admitting to an ulterior motive in the pursuit of his scientific studies. In a letter to Fleiss written at the very time that the dream book was "finished in all essentials,"[2] we read: "I see you are using the circuitous route of medicine to attain your first ideal, the physiological understanding of man, while I secretly nurse the hope of arriving by the same route at my own original objective, philosophy."[3] A few months later the same confession recurs in somewhat revised form. "When I was young, the only thing I longed for was philosophical knowledge, and now that I am going over from medicine to psychology, I am in the process of attaining it."[4] What prompted this circuitous route to the satisfaction of philosophical impulses, and what in writing *The Interpretation of Dreams* made him feel that he was attaining philosophical knowledge, Freud leaves unclear. But his attitude toward metaphysics provides, I think, some essential clues.

In *The Interpretation of Dreams* Freud felt it necessary to make an unambiguous disclaimer of metaphysical intent. The context is a polemical one in which Freud attacks the "prevailing trend of thought in psychiatry today," according to which "anything that might indicate that mental life is in any way independent of demonstrable organic changes or that its manifestations are in any way spontaneous" provokes alarm. "Even when investigation has shown that the primary exciting cause of a phenomenon is psychical," we are assured, "deeper research will one day trace the path further and discover an organic basis [*Begründung*] for the mental event." In the meantime, to grant mental impulses "means of their own" does not commit one to "the metaphysical view of the nature of the mind [*dem metaphysischen Seelenwesen*]."[5]

I would perhaps be hard pressed to establish the connection between Freud's dissociation of psychoanalytic understanding from metaphysics and his sense that *The Interpretation of Dreams* was carrying him via the circuitous route of natural science to the satisfaction of philosophical yearnings were it not for the fact that Freud himself establishes that connection. In *The Psychopathology of Everyday Life* (1901), a book otherwise devoid of speculative content, we suddenly encounter a striking and incisive expression of the "spiritual" orientation of psychoanalytic thought. Here metaphysics is equated, not with the philosophical tradition originating with Plato, but with the religious "Platonism for the people" (Nietzsche) that was absorbed into the conceptual framework of that tradition.

> A large part of the mythological view of the world, which extends a long way into the most modern religions, *is nothing but psychology projected into the external world*. The obscure recognition . . . of psychical factors and relations in the unconscious is mirrored—it is difficult to express it in other terms, and here the analogy with paranoia must come to our aid—in the construction of a *supernatural reality*, which is destined to be changed back once more by science into the *psychology of the unconscious*. One could venture to explain in this way the myths of paradise and the fall of man, of God, of good and evil, of immortality, and so on, and to transform *metaphysics* into *metapsychology*. [Freud's italics][6]

The transformation of metaphysics into metapsychology must not be confused with the dismissal of metaphysical concerns as meaningless, typical, for instance, of the logical positivism of the Vienna Circle.[7] In this transformation Freud does not merely jettison metaphysics as some kind of colossal linguistic blunder. On the contrary, as the reflection of psychical factors in the unconscious, metaphysics becomes the mirror in which the mind might seek the image of its own innermost reality. The ultimate aim of the psychology of the unconscious is to fulfill the scientifically ordained destiny of metaphysics by transforming it into metapsychology. In the letter to Fleiss where Freud adumbrates the groundwork of psychoanalytic theory, we saw how he used the term metapsychology to signify the organic, which he locates at a level both behind and beneath the psychological. Now, in his first published use of the term (then dropped until the "Metapsychological Papers" of 1915), Freud situates metapsychology in polar opposition to metaphysics. Yet the original biological meaning of the term is still latent in this new formulation. For what ultimately sustain metaphysical illusions are the urgent needs welling up from within, which the wishful impulses populating the unconscious represent.

Freud's formulations encode another meaning. In them, he announces the destiny science has ordained for the transcendental truths portended by myth and religion. But he also betrays the fate that had befallen his own philosophical impulses. Deflected from visions of a higher world by Darwin's enfolding of mind within nature, those impulses had but one recourse were they to find satisfaction. Forced by science to disavow metaphysics, Freud became the instrument of science. By the same token, science became his instrument—the vehicle for a philosophical quest. If the penetrating glare of science exposed the truths portended by myth and religion to be illusions, those illusions nonetheless point to the darkest layers of human subjectivity, the deepest wishes of the human heart, the essential nature of the human animal. By treating the metaphysical answers to the ultimate questions of existence as unconscious manifestations of human psychology, Freud could hope to translate transcendental illusions into scientific truths, to capture the human essence within the cognitions of science.

The psychology of the unconscious established in the founding movements of psychoanalytic theory is not itself, however, the transformation of metaphysics into metapsychology. By the very logic of Freud's endeavor, it could not be. It was science that had ordained the destiny of metaphysics. To become the instrument of science, Freud had first to forge that instrument—which is to say, his own understanding—within the crucible of science, to articulate a psychology that would carry the authority of science. In order for metaphysics to be changed back *by science* into the psychology of the unconscious, Freud had first to be in possession of the psychology of the unconscious *as* a science. Only when he had this completed instrument in hand could he apply it to metaphysics and disclose the realities of human being that are reflected in the mirror of metaphysics.

Although Freud would not pursue this ambition until, some eleven years later, he came to write *Totem and Taboo* (1912–13), its formulation nonetheless stands as an important signpost on the way of his thought. *Flectere si nequeo superos, Acheronta movebo* ("If I cannot bend the Higher Powers, I will stir up the Underworld") was the motto Freud chose for the dream book. And, without contradicting his explanation that this motto represents the course taken by repressed wishes that, rejected by consciousness, find their expression in dreams,[8] it can also be understood to represent the course taken by Freud's youthful philosophical passions in the recognition that the triumph natural science won through Darwin had foreclosed access to the metaphysical realm—the realm where, traditionally, mind found in philosophical knowledge "its realization," as Hegel tells us, "and the kingdom it sets up for itself in its own native element."[9] As metaphysics reflected back into its origins, metapsychology became for Freud the new source of transcendent meaning. Or, rather, as a response to the enfolding of the mind within nature, the transformation of metaphysics into metapsychology substitutes an immanent "within" for a transcendent "beyond" as the ground of self-understanding.

The foregoing considerations are meant to establish that Freud's materialism arises out of his disavowal of metaphysics—a disavowal that gives definitive form to the new vision of human reality Freud tries to elaborate in the aftermath of metaphysics. Let me not be misunderstood. I am not implying that Freud's orientation toward biology via his opposition to metaphysics somehow saves metaphysics. On the contrary, my point is that Freud's stirring up of the underworld, his reflective elaborations of our creaturely nature, upon whose repudiation metaphysics had always stood, seeks to make the end of metaphysics irrevocable by fulfilling natural science's claim to account for the totality of the existent. *Totem and Taboo* only consummates the disavowal of metaphysics that is already implicit in the founding of psychoanalysis. Its final words, taken from Goethe's

Faust, are " 'in the beginning was the Deed.' "[10] Those words constitute, among other things, a repudiation of the Platonism of the Fourth Gospel. Moreover, in tracing the genesis of religion to the psychohistorical dynamics of Darwin's primal horde, *Totem and Taboo* also gives a natural scientific answer to what Kant posed as the first question of metaphysics—namely, *"How is metaphysics, as natural disposition, possible?"*[11]

In bringing metaphysics to a close on behalf of natural science, however, Freud also saw that mind had to be assimilated back into nature without excluding thereby the immediate self-certainty of being, which is the irreducible datum of every human life. In this context we can begin to see how the grounding operation represents the seminal, constitutive act in a movement of mind of greater proportions. We must now try to gain a closer understanding of what is involved in that movement by considering more fully how Darwinism simultaneously foreclosed access to metaphysics and opened up the possibility of reconstituting a comprehensive vision of man as *homo natura.*

Darwinism and the Dissolution of the Metaphysical Equation

If my concern were simply to show that Freud was deeply influenced by evolutionary thought, I would certainly have done better to cite Lamarck rather than Darwin as decisive for the development of psychoanalytic theory. After *Totem and Taboo* Freud became an adherent to one version of Lamarck's views concerning the nature of the evolutionary process.[12] In particular, Freud found the Lamarckian mechanism of evolution through the inheritance of acquired characteristics a necessary assumption for the articulation of his theory of human phylogenesis. But, in fact, Freud did not introduce the inheritance of acquired characteristics into psychoanalytic theory because he was influenced by Lamarckism. On the contrary, he came to embrace Lamarckism for *psychoanalytic* reasons that we shall explore at a later point. In any case, our fundamental thesis— that psychoanalysis elaborates the meaning of Darwinism for human self-understanding—does not refer to the influence of evolutionism on Freud's thought. The treatment of a great thinker's work in terms of a history of influences, however useful in familiarizing us with his intellectual environment, can never succeed in revealing the theoretical passion that consumes itself in the life of his thought. Whatever its appropriations and whatever its failings, Freud's thought is original. That is, it poses and answers the essential questions for itself rather than merely adopting a ready-made viewpoint, methodology, or set of assumptions. The fundamental thesis is meant to indicate the originality of psychoanalysis as a solution to the enigma evolution posed for self-understanding—as a convoluted but internally consistent response to the question man became for himself in the wake of Darwin.

A concern for the historical impact of evolutionary science is what led Freud to cite Darwin and not Lamarck in his discussion of the "three blows" dealt to human narcissism by the researches of science, even though when he wrote the article discussing the matter he had already come to consider Lamarck's work, which preceded Darwin's, to be scientifically more valid. For it was because of Darwin's impact that the natural sciences had come to fully dominate the human mind. This meant, moreover, that the consequences of evolutionism for human self-understanding would have to be worked out in accordance with the ontological blueprint projected by the natural sciences, although Darwinism itself, as we shall see, added a new dimension to that blueprint. What I am arguing is that, read as a response to the new situation of understanding created by Darwinism, psychoanalysis becomes a prism that enables us to see the elementary theoretical questions that animated Freud and made him a seminal architect of the modern sensibility.

More particularly, in the context of our current discussion, Freud's recourse from metaphysics to natural history attests to the closure of the metaphysical horizon in which evolution played a decisive role. For Darwinism fundamentally disturbed the constitutive equation of the metaphysical tradition and thus threw into disarray the light of understanding which that equation had kept in focus. It was into this situation that psychoanalysis stepped, in order to provide what Freud claimed was "a decisive new orientation in the world and in science."[13] In disavowing metaphysics and turning to natural history for the determination of the human essence, Freud's philosophical daimon showed a rudimentary grasp of, and turned to its advantage, the dissolutive impact of evolution on the interpretation of man handed down by the metaphysical tradition through reflective philosophy.

The constitutive equation of the metaphysical tradition, insofar as it bears on human self-understanding, is contained in the nexus Plato and Aristotle established between man, mind, and being. Psychoanalytic thought does not stand in direct relationship with ancient philosophy. Nonetheless, Freud's thought engages and overturns from within the interpretation of man that took shape in the metaphysical tradition as it got handed down to the modern age by reflective philosophy. Descartes, who founded reflective philosophy, took up the mantle of metaphysics in the wake of the discoveries of Copernicus and Galileo. Reflective philosophy is a crisis metaphysics whose historic task has been to sustain a modus vivendi between the epistemic claims of the new science of nature and the ontological insights of the older philosophic tradition.

In that ancient tradition, the essence of man is both located by philosophy and found to stand in an intimate relation with the philosophical activity itself. To put matters summarily, reason is what is highest in man, and the way of philosophy is life in accordance with reason. In its purest form, philosophy is what we have come to call metaphysics. Metaphysics seeks after a timeless reality that stands behind the transient appearances through reason's grasp of the highest principles of being. Coming to be in the contemplative vision of what changelessly is, mind finds its truth in the truth of being.

The needs and passions of life, however, disturb the contemplative suspension of time, thereby disqualifying philosophy as a way of life for the many. Instead, and here we follow Aristotle's line of thought, the many are assigned politics as the sphere of activity for the actualization of their rational faculties. The actualization of the human essence in ethico-political action is authentic, however—and here Plato and Aristotle agree in their diversity—only to the extent that it conforms to the standards set by philosophy itself.

"Consciousness," Heidegger once remarked, "is the land of modern metaphysics."[14] Upon this land the essentials of the ancient equation of man, mind, and being are reasserted in the philosophies of Kant and Hegel. Again, mind finds its realization in the comprehension of being. And again, the essence of man finds its worldly manifestation in the sphere of ethico-political action under the supervision of philosophy. But the contemplation of being is complicated by the grounding of reason in the self—a complication whose ramifications in the philosophies of Descartes, Kant, and Hegel we can hardly do justice here. Instead, we shall focus on one manifestation of that complication in the philosophy of Hegel.

Making its starting point on the hither side of Descartes's dualism, the *Phenomenology of Mind* tries to absorb the antithetical presence of otherness by a dialectical movement of mind Hegel calls the "Science of the Experience of Consciousness."[15]

> In pressing forward to its true form of existence, consciousnes will come to a point at which it lays aside its semblance of being hampered with what is foreign to it, with what is only for it and exists as another; it will reach a position where appearance becomes identified with essence, where, in consequence, its exposition coincides with just this very point, this very stage of the science proper of mind. And finally, when it grasps this its own essence, it will connote the nature of absolute knowledge itself.[16]

Yet the summative proposition of this effort—the proposition that "Substance is Subject"[17]—attests to Hegel's ultimate inability to overcome the consequences of the Copernican revolution for metaphysics. Instead, Hegel's thought becomes philosophy's unwitting confession. Forced to a recognition of its own essence by the Copernican revolution, philosophy discloses the being of metaphysics to be reflection itself. Thus, in Hegel's *Philosophy of Nature*, the material world, while in principle the externalization of Spirit, in fact remains a presence forever external to mind—a situation no amount of reflective mediation can remedy. As Marx noted in his *Paris Manuscripts*, "Philosophy . . . has remained just as alien to [the natural sciences] as they remain to philosophy. Their momentary unity was only a *chimerical illusion*. The will was there, but the power was lacking."[18]

Darwin's *Origin of Species* (1859), which established the evolution of life as a scientific fact, fundamentally altered the epistemic situation upon which the traditional interpretation of man rested. By bringing into view a self-generating nature out of whose contingent yet causally determined interactional processes man appears as but one more product, evolution was the instrument by which natural science finally forced the issue with metaphysics. Consciousness, the land of modern metaphysics, was denied metaphysical paternity and its special relationship with human life. If we take evolution seriously as embracing the phenomenon of man, which in some sense we must, then mind ceases to represent an independent ontological substance that realizes itself in the act of reflection, but instead must be understood to have emerged from matter as the actualization of some potentiality inherent therein.[19] Reason can no longer be assigned the task of realizing the human essence by subordinating the passions of life to standards determined by the philosopher's perception of being. For evolution makes reason an attribute of life rather than its master. Finally, absolute being, insofar as it is still identified with what timelessly is, dissolves into nothingness in the face of the temporality that evolution implants at the very heart of everything that exists. "If there is nothing eternal," Aristotle notes in his *Metaphysics*, "then there can be no becoming: for there must be something which undergoes the process of becoming."[20] From a Darwinian standpoint, however, coming-to-be does not arise from what eternally is. Rather, all discrete entities derive their being from becoming. Becoming is now the superior principle—or, rather, in the face of the primacy and universality of process and change, the whole distinction between being and becoming loses efficacy and significance. For in becoming, entities proceed from an origin, but toward no final state, and realize no purposes. Their ontological meaning is fully exhausted in the determination of the causes that have produced them.

Darwinism and Temporality

We have reached the point where we can pass from a consideration of the dissolutive impact of Darwinism upon metaphysics to a positive accounting of the ontological regime that evolution institutes in its stead. The reflections of Hans Jonas, which have been instrumental to this point, will also form the starting point for this new task, but this time in the context of an interpretative disagreement. Impressed by the nihilistic consequences evolution bears for the philosophical tradition, Jonas skillfully develops those implications to the point where Darwinism is forced to confess its limitations, thereby restoring philosophical reflection to its rights. In the process, however, Jonas overlooks certain novel aspects of the meaning of Darwinism for science. Jonas sees evolution as clinching natural science's case for unlimited sovereignty over what is by embracing life within the ontological scheme already implicit in its Copernican-Galilean origins. This leads him to neglect the dimension of the nature evolution brings into view that was not anticipated in those origins—the dimension, that is, of temporality. This dimension enables the psychoanalytic interpretation of man to restore the sense of essentialism without the support of metaphysics. In its encounter with the unforeseen, evolution looks forward beyond the Newtonian regime as well as backward to its origins.

Jonas teaches us that Darwin's success in establishing a mechanical explanation for the origins and development of living beings "completed the Copernican revolution in ontology" by extending "to the realm of *life* that combination of natural necessity with radical contingency which the Newtonian-Laplacean cosmology resulting from that revolution had universally proclaimed."[21] By calling Darwinism the *completion* of the Copernican revolution in ontology, Jonas means to signify the claim science could now make upon the totality of the existent—a totality conceived monistically as matter. For evolution treats the vital difference between the organic and the inorganic in mechanical terms as the emergence of the simplest self-replicating structures from random encounters and transmutations within nonvital matter. Random variations in the offspring and the natural selection of those that best suit the organism for survival then account for the further course of development. The elements of radical contingency essential to the ontological blueprint of nature that science projects is secured in Darwin's theory by the fact that variation is a function of the organism and natural selection a function of the environment. The two functions, that is, originate independently or, at least, no conspiracy of nature coordinates organic and environmental changes so as to realize some preordained pattern of development. On the other hand, the natural necessity Jonas cites as the second element of the Newtonian-Laplacean cosmology is operative in the nonpurposive "selection" of the fittest through the elimination of those organisms relatively deficient in the equipment for survival within an externally given environment. Necessity is at work here in the stark alternatives of life and death, being and nonbeing.

If this were the sum total of the matter, it would be difficult to understand how Freud managed to bring human evidences into conformity with the ground plan of nature projected by evolutionary science. But here psychoanalysis directs us to an aspect of evolution's meaning for science that Jonas overlooks. This aspect is essential to the comprehension of now the Freudian interpretation of man manages to restore the sense of essentialism while conforming to the specifications on science's blueprint of nature, as evolution had modified it. By Jonas's account, Darwin's achievement consisted in his explanation of the evolution of living entities within the Newtonian causal scheme signified by the combination of natural necessity and radical contingency—a causal scheme whose cosmological implications were developed by Laplace. Darwinism, however, did more than just conquer the realm of life for the Newtonian world view. By that very act, evolution transformed the role which natural science assigned to time in the scheme of things. The conquest of vital existence for a mechanistic natural science was thus exacted at an unexpected price. The organic beings that were now subjected to the rigors of efficient causality bore within themselves something which radicalized that causal scheme. Evolutionary science thereby inserted into the ground plan of nature something that Freud could turn to his advantage in reconstituting a coherent vision of man after his fall from metaphysical grace.

In his analysis of the Darwinian causal scheme, and of its conformity with the Newtonian-Laplacean cosmology, Jonas neglects the distinctive meaning that evolutionism imparts to time. He turns to Laplace's "hypothetical 'divine Calculator' "[22] for the cosmological expression of systemic change in Newtonian physics. This hypothesis illustrates most vividly the significance of time within that understanding of nature. But in his discussion of Laplace's hypothesis, Jonas fails to note the ironic twist Darwin gives to it.

Laplace's famous hypothesis runs as follows:

> An intellect which at a given instant knows all the forces acting in nature and the position of all things of which the world consists—supposing said intellect were vast enough to subject these data to analysis—would embrace in the same formula the motions of the greatest bodies in the universe and those of the slightest atoms; nothing would be uncertain for it, and the future like the past would be present to its eyes.[23]

The vision of natural processes given here is such that, in the words of Milič Čapek, "any instantaneous configuration of an isolated system logically implies all future configurations of the system. Its future history is thus virtually contained in its present state, which, in turn is logically contained in its past states."[24] For Jonas, Laplace's hypothesis complements Newton's mechanical explanation of "existing structures" by extending those mechanics to the question of origins and development,[25] thereby filling out and elevating to the level of cosmology the vision of the new natural science—a vision whose "metaphysical secret," Jonas notes, lies "in a radically temporal conception of being, or in its identification with action and process."[26] It is into this scheme, then, that, for Jonas, Darwin fits the realm of life. But what Jonas fails to see is that, with the capturing of life phenomena within the explanatory net of efficient causality, the concept of time contained in natural science's "radically temporal conception of being" is itself radicalized. Let us see how.

In its abstention from teleological explanation, the interaction of variation and natural selection is in complete agreement with the Newtonian-Laplacean cosmology. Indeed, Darwin's explanation of organic phenomena without recourse to teleology is perhaps the most concise expression of the victory natural science won through him over metaphysics. For in living things, philosophy had one class of entities whose teleological nature appeared to be indisputable. Kant, no enemy of Newtonianism, thought that the principle of teleology was essential to any science of "organized beings."[27] Thus Darwin's elimination of teleology from its refuge in living nature was of great significance. As John Dewey noted, "the combination of the very words origin and species [in Darwin's title] embodied an intellectual revolt." For in its traditional philosophical usage, which originates with Aristotle, species *(eidos)* represented the "formal activity which operates throughout the series of changes and holds them to a single course; which subordinates their aimless flux to its own perfect manifestation; which leaping the boundaries of time and space, keeps individuals distant in space and remote in time to a uniform type of structure and function."[28]

The eradication of teleology was accomplished, however, by the radicalization of its opposite, contingency, and with peculiar consequences. In Laplace's vision the chain of causality can be reckoned backward and forward. "The direction of time," Čapek notes, "has hardly any meaning in rational mechanics."[29] The reversal of time is simply a matter of mathematical manipulation in which a plus sign is changed to a minus sign. Time, being infinite, continuous, and uniform, is but a "mathematically measurable duration"[30] which, like Newtonian space, remains external to the events that transpire in it. Contingency refers only to the arbitrariness of the initial set of conditions—the first configuration of the system that, once set in motion, unfolds within the grid of absolute time and space with ineluctable necessity. Since all relations are isometric, this world system can be read backward or forward with equal sense.

None of this holds true in Darwin's theory of evolution, where the role of contingency is expanded dramatically. In the evolution of life, contingency is at work at every significant turning point in development, without thereby abrogating the law of necessity. Indeed, the unpredictable irruption of new organic forms is exactly what constitutes these important turning points. For evolution signifies the emergence of novel and unexpected adaptations out of the interplay of random organic mutations and changed organic and inorganic conditions of life. In the theory of evolution no future state of the system is given with certainty in the present configuration. The present generation of a particular species is the cumulative product of the movement of life through time, and is thereby its effect. But while the variations that the present generation throws out through its offspring for natural selection condition future possibilities, just what those variations will be and with what result, given changed environmental conditions, cannot be determined beforehand. To put it another way, the life or death selection lottery held every generation for the members of every species allows us in principle to infer that a rigorous causal sequence accounts for the current state of the natural economy. But the cumulative, causally determined emergence of new biological forms describes a developmental trajectory that is, by nature, irreversible. "Time's arrow" points in one direction only—and that is forward to a future which, once realized, will be seen to have been determined by the past, but whose definitive outcome remains hidden to the eyes of the present.

For the idea of time implicit in the evolutionary development of life disclosed by Darwin's causal scheme, I would reserve the word temporality. Temporality is found not in the mathematical interval that makes up the uniform, continuous, and infinite time used by Newton to measure bodies in motion but rather in the event which forms part of the unique sequence of happenings that make up the story of life. Thus Darwin informs us in the *Origin of Species* that, for evolutionary understanding, "we regard every production of nature as one which has had a history" and that "every complex structure and instinct" is to be understood as "the summing up" of the species history of the organism possessing it.[31] With the theory of evolution, the vision of time projected by the natural sciences ceases to be monopolized by Newtonian mechanics. Evolutionary time does not derive its fundamental characteristics from the mathematics of masses in motion. As put sharply by François Jacob, "Living bodies are indissolubly bound up with time. In the living world, no structure can be detached from its history."[32] For evolution, time is not merely a measure applied to organic entities from without. It is of their essence.

This element of temporality, which Darwinism inserted into the ground plan of nature, is what Freudian theory exploits in order to restore the sense of essentialism in the context of natural history. But in order to see how this is so, we must explore more deeply the nature and implications of temporality in evolutionary theory. So far, the temporality we have spoken of pertains solely to species. The story of life on earth is the story of a single, continuous development characterized by the increasing complexity of life forms through the diversification into species of an original protoplasm. What evolve are species. But they evolve through the individual organisms in which each species has its empirical reality. As the most recent product of the immense journey of life through time, individual organisms are thus the concrete manifestations of the temporality of life. Every complex structure or instinct is the summing up of the organism's species history because, in the theory of evolution, the individual organism is conceptually subordinate to the history of its species. This relationship of organism to species helps explain the seductive logic of Haeckel's famous "biogenetic law," which Freud adopts as the logic linking the psychical development of the individual to the development of civilization in *Totem and Taboo*.

Haeckel's biogenetic law—which, put briefly, asserts that ontogeny recapitulates phylogeny—is no longer taken seriously by most biologists, even though recapitulation theory was the explanation of individual organic development favored by Darwin.[33] The facts of ontogenetic development (ontogeny being understood variously to signify embryological and/or anatomical development of the individual organism) simply do not conform to its logic. Nonetheless, recapitulation theory dominated the first generation of post-Darwinian biologists because, as we shall see, it idealizes the ontological implications that the theory of evolution bears for individual organisms. Since our concern is with how psychoanalysis elaborates the meaning of Darwinism for human self-understanding, Haeckel's idealization helps us see what possibilities for reconstituting a coherent vision of human reality were available when nature was viewed from the rudimentary perspective Darwin established.

We begin with Haeckel's own formulation of the law of recapitulation.

> Ontogeny, or the development of the individual, being the series of form-changes which each individual organism traverses during the whole time of its individual existence, is immediately conditioned by phylogeny, or the development of the organic stock (phylon) to which it belongs.

> Ontogeny is the short and rapid recapitulation of phylogeny, conditioned by the physiological functions of heredity (reproduction) and adaptation (mutation). The organic individual . . . repeats during the rapid and short course of its individual development the most important form-changes which its ancestors traversed during the long and slow course of their paleontological evolution according to the laws of heredity and adaptation.[34]

The biogenetic law pertains to a developmental process that the *Origin of Species* is largely unconcerned with—namely, the development of the individual organism. But why then was the biogenetic law so appealing to Darwinists as a way of explaining the development of the individual organism? The answer is that if the law were true, it would provide an invaluable guide to the generation of phylogenetic sequences—sequences that the incompleteness of the fossil record makes so difficult in many cases to reconstruct. But prior to the question of usefulness and appeal comes the question of what made recapitulation theory so *plausible* as the proper interpretation or explanation of individual development. The answer lies in evolutionary science's elimination of teleology from the realm of living things.

One aspect of the elimination of teleology lay in Darwin's treatment of what Charles Gillispie has called the "crucial problem of adaptation."

> Crucial it was, because the case in favor of purpose, the conception of biology as the science of the goal-directed, rested precisely there, on the ancient and reasonable observation that animals seem to be made in order to fit their circumstances and in order to lead the lives they do lead, with the right equipment, the right instincts and the right habits.

Darwin did better than solve the problem of adaptation. He abolished it. He turned it from a cause, in the sense of final cause or evidence of a designing purpose, into an effect, which is to say that adaptation became a fact or phenomenon to be analyzed, rather than a mystery to be plumbed.[35]

Gillispie makes an acute point. By taking adaptation as a given datum, Darwin could pose the question of what produced it as his causal problem, to which he provided a nonteleological answer in the obvious fact that what is not adapted perishes. This fact is no less efficacious for being tautological—the tautology here saved from inanity by evolutionary science's inability to predict what future adaptations will look like.

Important as all this may be, it does not take us to the heart of the connection between Haeckel's biogenetic law and the elimination of teleology in the evolutionary conception of life. Actually, Gillispie has overstated his case in saying that pre-Darwinian biology, as the science of the goal-directed, rested on the ancient perception of the adaptation of organisms to their environment. Insofar as the category of teleology is concerned, another aspect of the apparent purposefulness manifest in living things was far more important, at least to the most influential articulator of that category, Aristotle. John Dewey expresses eloquently how matters appeared to Greek eyes, although it is clearly the eyes of the founder of the Lyceum that are made their representative.

> The changes in living things are orderly; they are cumulative; they tend constantly in one direction; they do not, like other changes, destroy or consume, or pass fruitless into wandering flux; they realize and fulfill. Each successive stage, no matter how unlike its predecessor, preserves its net effect and also prepares the way for a further activity on the part of its successor. In living beings, changes do not happen as they seem to happen elsewhere, any which way; the earlier changes are regulated in view of later results. This progressive organization does not cease till there is achieved a true final term, a *telos*, a completed, perfected end.[36]

To reverse matters, Aristotle's notion of teleology found in the growth of living things, as it still does for our common-sense understanding, its most persuasive experiential referent.

Consider, then, the implications Darwinism bears for the teleological understanding of what is entailed in the series of form changes through which the organism passes. To Greek eyes, each organism's coming-to-be represented the step-by-step unfolding of an essential nature. The process of becoming was intelligible by virtue of a subordination to its final state of being. Let us remember that the original use of the term species signified just this unchanging, eternally fixed form which each organism, in its growth, strives to realize. With evolution, the individual organism ceases to be the manifestation-through-a-process-of-becoming of a fixed species nature. For species itself represents a developmental sequence of generations, through aeons of the past, whose future course is unknown. With relation to its species, the individual living organism represents this past history for the present, and is the bearer of what the species thus is for the present on its path toward a contingency-filled future. Thus, even though a species exists only through the succession of organisms that make it up, the species, by the logic of evolution, nonetheless subordinates the individual living organism to its species history and imparts to the living organism the character of a concretion of historical time. By conceiving of the sequence of form changes through which the organism passes as the step-by-step repetition of its species history, Haeckel's law makes evolutionary time the form in which the organism lives out its lifetime. Instead of representing the teleological striving to embody an eternal form of being, the organism follows Goethe's advice and realizes the historical past as its own destiny. The ontological meaning of the organism is not contained in the form it realizes but in the sequence of form changes through which it passes. The temporality of the species is the "essence" of the organism.

Haeckel's biogenetic law, as we have said, has proved to be fallacious, although interestingly enough it is still considered to be of heuristic value. The reason, I think, is obvious. The constitution of a phylogenetic series from fossil remains requires, among other things, the ability to imagine a series of incremental changes by which some simple corporeal structure has developed into one of great complexity. The theory of evolution requires us to consider the multiplicity of life, in all its complex diversity, as having evolved from some simple, elementary progenitor. In the development of an embryo from a single cell, biology finds a dramatic model to which it can turn for guidance. "Embryology is to me," Darwin wrote the year after *Origin of Species* was published, "by far the strongest single class of facts in favor of change of forms."[37] The appeal of embryology to the propounder of descent with modification is revealing here. For not only does embryology, whose mechanics are still a mystery to science, offer the fascinating spectacle of the emergence of a highly complex organism from a single cell, it has the distinct advantage of ending not in some final form but with birth—with the beginning, that is, of another process of progressive development. In this, the self-contained series of embryological changes also permits the observer to ignore that pattern of form changes which remains opaque or, at least, irrelevant to the evolutionary understanding: passing away, senescence, and decay.

In the absence of teleology, then, Haeckel's biogenetic law was a plausible guess at the nature of ontogeny (a word, incidentally, that he coined) which proved wrong. But this in itself does not speak against the significance of recapitulation theory as an idealization of the temporality that still inheres in the ground plan of nature projected by evolutionary science. The abandonment of the biogenetic law in no way affected either the validity of Darwin's theory of evolution or the status of the individual organism as the summing up of its species history, which recapitulation theory attempted to formalize.

What concerns us here is that Haeckel's law brings into high relief the form of time which, for evolution, belongs to living nature. In its explication of the temporality that, after Darwin, inheres in the form of every discrete organism, Haeckel's law gives us insight into Freud's attempt to discover the sense of being what we are—creatures who by origin and destiny belong to nature. This insight is to be found, not by attending to Freud's explicit adoption of the biogenetic law in the anthropology of *Totem and Taboo*, but rather by comprehending his reconstruction of the human essence in accordance with that aspect of evolutionary understanding that the biogenetic law explicates—by seeing, that is, how psychoanalytic reflection realizes within human self-understanding the temporality that evolutionary science makes part of living nature's substance. "Impressive analogies from biology," Freud writes in the Leonardo study of 1910, "have prepared us to find that the individual's mental development repeats the course of human development in an abbreviated form."[38] It is only because the temporality projected by evolutionary science had already been incorporated by the grounding operation into Freud's vision of human reality that these analogies could open the way to the generation of a cultural anthropology out of his individual psychology. Thus we must return to the level of individual psychology.

CHAPTER 7

The Psychoanalytic Understanding of Life

"The basic text of *homo natura* must again be recognized," Nietzsche urges in *Beyond Good and Evil*. "To translate man back into nature"—that is the task of the contemporary thinker who, "hardened by the discipline of science," is at last "deaf to the siren songs of old metaphysical bird catchers who have been piping at him too long, you are more, you are higher, you are of a different origin."[1] In the grounding operation Freud carries out that task. *The Interpretation of Dreams* inaugurates the era of psychoanalytic man, of man left with nothing but life itself and whatever sense he can make of it. But psychoanalytic man is not yet existential man. The discovery that there is nothing beyond life is not for Freud the occasion for existential despair and for the resolve to be in the face of life's absurdity. Thrown back upon life by science, psychoanalytic man is by the same token delivered to science for the interpretation of life. And for science, life is not an absurdity. Life is a complex and unexpected achievement in the career of matter.

This achievement has no meaning for the immediate experience of life. But, whatever his doubts and anxieties, psychoanalytic man knows that the life he lives does not hang suspended over an existential void. For beneath life stands the rich multiplicity of nature, from which life arises and to which it returns. By translating man back into nature, Freud attempts to make the nature envisioned by science the basis for human self-understanding. That translation takes the form of a recourse from the metaphysical view of the nature of the mind to an elaboration of the mind's natural history. We are now in a position to show how Freud's elaboration of the human essence takes place in this new setting.

The transcendence of time is the ancient dream of metaphysics. Metaphysics tries to fulfill that dream by permeating the world with thought in accordance with its requirements. In the *Metaphysics* Aristotle finds that "the principles of eternal things are necessarily the most true; for they are true always and not merely sometimes; and there is nothing which explains their being what they are, for it is they that explain the being of others. Consequently, status in being governs status in truth."[2] In eternal things lies the essence of entities—the substance that persists in and through all changes any particular things undergoes, insofar as it remains what it is and does not become something else. Psychoanalysis, we said, undertakes to reconstitute a vision of human reality in accordance with a perception of its essence, and to do this despite natural science's dissolution of being, of teleology, of the realm of final ends, and its subjection of everything that is to the rigors of efficient causality, to the relentless motion of sheer, purposeless becoming. The psychoanalytic interpretation of man finds the means by which to restore the sense of essentialism in evolutionary science's insertion of temporality into the ground plan of nature. Let us see how.

Temporality is time that is lived forward but comprehended backward. But this does not make temporality merely a subjective, psychological phenomenon. As evolutionary biology is fully cognizant, living things are themselves already temporal, that is, conditioned by time. Temporality here does not signify a parameter of measurement for living things but is a property of their being per se. Having discovered the temporal nature of species and disclosed the mechanism of their progressive development and differentiation, evolutionary biology imparts a determinate meaning to discrete living entities by treating each as the summation of a species history. In doing this, evolution frees organic time from its subordination to the teleology of an eternally fixed species form. As we saw, Haeckel's biogenetic law tries to render the lifetime of an individual organism perspicuous as the concrete embodiment of the species' history. Haeckel thereby idealizes the meaning borne by evolution for the individual organism. That meaning is that the nature of the organism is contained in the history of the species—a history which, for contemporary evolutionary theory, the organism inherits in its genetic endowment. That is to say, *the past itself takes the place of the superordinate fixed form which the organism strives to become.*

Because of its concern with the archeology of the subject, this orientation toward the past is the means through which psychoanalysis realizes the essence of man as desire. How it does so we can learn by turning to the Freudian work that teaches us the most about the meaning psychoanalytic theory imparts to the understanding of life, *Leonardo da Vinci and a Memory of His Childhood* (1910). That life transpires in time and that making sense of a life requires the exercise of memory (in the case of autobiography) or the imaginative reenactment of a life through strict adherence to chronology (in the case of biography) are hardly revelations. But that what a person shows in his life is to be understood in "the connection along the path of instinctual activity between a person's external experiences and his reactions"[3] is a claim distinctive to psychoanalysis—a claim whose possibilities and limitations Freud explores in his study of Leonardo. In the process we learn much about the view of life that issues from the grounding operation and about what reconstructing the experience of life into a natural history involves.[4]

Leonardo da Vinci and a Memory of His Childhood is clearly conceived as the application of the logic of psychosexual development, worked out in the *Three Essays,* to a concrete case. What Freud wants to account for is Leonardo's overwhelming passion for research and knowledge, and the particular forms this passion took in the course of his career both as an artist and as an investigator of nature. But psychobiography does not simply take the conditions, events, and actions of a person's life and develop them into a coherent story such that the meaning of that life is somehow allowed to speak for itself. Rather, psychobiography subjects those biographical data to a critical analysis of a special kind.

> Supported by its knowledge of psychical mechanisms, psycho-analytic enquiry endeavors to establish a dynamic basis for his nature on the strength of his reactions [to external events] and to disclose the original motive forces of his mind, as well as their later transformations and development. If this is successful the behavior of a personality in the course of his life is explained in terms of the combined operation of constitution and fate, of internal forces and external powers.[5]

The essence of a person's nature must be sought along the path of instinctual activity, which leads back to the original motive forces of the mind. Just as in biology, where genotypic characters manifest themselves phenotypically according to the conditions under which the organism's life transpires, so these "original motive forces" are manifest as a particular psychical configuration according to the interaction of innate disposition with external experiences. As Freud puts it in the 1915 edition of the *Three Essays,* the relation between constitutional and accidental factors is cooperative and not mutually exclusive. "The constitutional factor must await experiences before it can make itself felt; the accidental factor must have a constitutional basis in order to come into operation."[6] Once established, however, the original configuration of infantile sexual impulses— which are polymorphic and autoerotic—forms the basis for all later developments.

What give a dynamic character to these developments are the wave of repression that covers over the efflorescence of sexual activity with an infantile amnesia, and the subsequent vicissitudes that the repressed instincts undergo during the period of latency. The human organism is transformed into a civilized human being during the latency period through the diversion of polymorphic sexual energies to other purposes, according to a variety of possibilities about which Freud is never quite clear or settled but which include sublimation and neurotic compulsiveness. Both the wave of repression that ends the period of infantile sexual activity and the subsequent forms of instinctual canalization are themselves constitutionally determined, and comprise for Freud the virtual mark of human speciation. Thus, already in the first edition of the *Three Essays,* we read,

> The fact that the onset of sexual development in human beings occurs in two phases, i.e., that the development is interrupted by the period of latency, seemed [in the foregoing] to call for particular notice. This appears to be one of the necessary conditions of the aptitude of men for developing a higher civilization, but also of their tendency to neurosis. So far as we know, nothing analogous is to be found in man's animal relatives. It would seem that the origin of this peculiarity of men must be looked for in the prehistory of the human species.[7]

Just as in evolutionary science, where the constitutional species-character the individual inherits is itself a product of time, so in psychoanalytic science Freud bids us look to events in human prehistory to account for the capacity for acculturation with which each human being is born. "Constitution," he wrote Else Voigtländer in 1911, ". . . is nothing but the sediment of experiences from a long line of ancestors."[8]

In psychoanalysis, then, the dynamic basis of each person's mind is to be found in the disclosure of its original motive forces, as well as their later transformations and development, both of which are understood to be manifestations of innate constitutional factors stirred into action by the particular circumstances of the person's life. This basis is not grasped immediately but is inferred from a consideration of the leading characteristics of his adult personality. Thus, to return to the Leonardo study, we find Freud beginning not with Leonardo's childhood memory but, just as he would in a clinical situation, with the manifestations of the artist's character in later life.

> If we reflect on the concurrence in Leonardo of his overpowerful instinct for research and the atrophy of his sexual life (which was restricted to what is called ideal [sublimated] homosexuality) we shall be disposed to claim him as a model instance of [the sublimated] type. The core of his nature, and the secret of it, would appear to be that after his curiosity had been activated in infancy in the service of sexual interests, he succeeded in sublimating the greater part of his libido into an urge for research.[9]

According to the logic of psychosexual development, the key to an individual's character is always contained in the original fixations of infantile sexual life. But that key comes into view only in retrospect, in the light of a given outcome. The essence of an individual character is identified, not with the *telos* or end against which the unfolding of the self is measured, but with origins, of which all subsequent manifestations of the self are an echo. Origins become the basis for rendering the course of a life intelligible as *the persistence of desire through time*. The constitutive role assigned origins enables Freud to reproduce, as a vision of personal destiny, the peculiar combination of necessity and contingency that generates the temporality informing evolutionary understanding.

> Everything to do with our life is chance, from our origin out of the meeting of spermatazoon and ovum onwards—chance which nevertheless has a share in the law and necessity of nature, and which merely lacks any connection with our wishes and illusions. The apportioning of the determining factors of our life between the 'necessities' of our constitution and the 'chances' of our childhood may still be uncertain in detail; but in general it is no longer possible to doubt the importance of precisely the first years of our childhood.[10]

What makes sense of the experiences that we each have been fated to live is the reflective grasp of the psychoanalytically disciplined memory. Oriented toward the fixations of the past in his confrontation with the contingencies of the present, psychoanalytic man finds himself permeated with time through and through. In the critical reconstruction of one's life story along the path of instinctual activity, the sense of essentialism is restored in the context of a natural history of the mind. Psychoanalysis thus finds a way of lending a meaning to being biological and of making that meaning the basis of self-understanding.

In subjecting inward experience to a psychoanalysis, Freud seeks to resolve the mind back into the historical vicissitudes of the body lived from within. In this way psychoanalysis unfolds the meaning of the animal essence of human existence within the understanding. For Freud psychoanalytic theory thus provides the proper self-understanding for the human species in the wake of evolutionary science. That meaning, insofar as evolution bears any such meaning, is that man is the self-awareness of nature's will-to-be. Thus, referring to the "obscure words" of Leonardo that "nature . . . 'is full of countless causes *('ragioni')* that never enter experience,' " Freud concludes his study with a revealing gloss on Leonardo's words: "Every one of us human beings corresponds to one of the countless experiments in which these 'ragioni' of nature force their way into experience."[11] After Darwin, this is the one metapsychological truth of which we can have no doubt.

Now the path of instinctual activity also describes the history of those wishful impulses which, having succumbed to the great wave of repression that terminates infantile sexual activity, comprise the nucleus of the unconscious. And, since the recourse to natural history takes place in preparation for the transformation of metaphysics into metapsychology, it is not surprising that in the "Metapsychological Papers" of 1915, Freud finally assigns to the unconscious the leading characteristic of metaphysical reality. "The processes of the system *Ucs.* are *timeless,* i.e., they are not ordered temporally, are not altered by the passage of time; they have no reference to time at all."[12] The persistence of desire through time expresses for Freud a will-to-be that transcends all discrete, time-bound manifestations of it. For Freud, let us remember, the originative moment of human psychical existence is the "experience of satisfaction." Psychoanalysis thus stands on the same ground as Whitehead's philosophy of organism, which in *Process and Reality* is given the following provocative articulation:

> The philosophy of organism is the inversion of Kant's philosophy. *The Critique of Pure Reason* describes the process by which subjective data pass into the appearance of an objective world. The philosophy of organism seeks to describe how objective data pass into subjective satisfaction. For Kant, the world emerges from the subject; for the philosophy of organism, the subject emerges from the world—a 'superject' rather than a 'subject'.[13]

In the case of psychoanalysis the "superject" secures a self out of the shifting contents of the object world by binding all subsequent experiences to an original one at whose restoration all psychical activity is aimed. The finding of an object, we learn in the paper on "Negation" (1925), is always a refinding of it.[14] This is the basis of the "timelessness" of the unconscious—a timelessness that is strangely finite since it is bound to the lifetime of the organism. In the constitutive role assigned the experience of satisfaction for psychogenesis, this basis is already laid out in the final chapter of *The Interpretation of Dreams*.

> An essential component of this experience of satisfaction is a particular perception (that of nourishment, in our example) the mnemic image of which remains associated thenceforward with the memory trace of the excitation produced by the need. As a result of the link that has thus been established, next time this need arises a psychical impulse will at once emerge which will seek to re-cathect the mnemic image of the perception and to re-evoke the perception itself, that is to say, to re-establish the situation of the original satisfaction. An impulse of this kind is what we call a wish; the re-appearance of the perception is the fulfilment of the wish.[15]

The path that the (ontogenetically) primitive mental apparatus follows, Freud asks us to assume, is one "in which wishing ended in hallucinating."[16] Or, as he puts it in the *Introductory Lectures,* "Every desire takes before long the form of picturing its own fulfilment."[17] That picturing leaves the realm of fantasy and takes the form of a hallucination when, as in the oneiric restoration of the mind's authentic originality, it takes itself to be an experience of reality. The timelessness of unconscious wishes, as opposed to the timelessness of Aristotle's "eternal things," does not connote a realm of being that stands beyond the transience of life. Metapsychological timelessness inheres in the experience of being organic realized by the psychoanalytic memory which, in tracing the continuity of desire through time, redeems a self from the transience of life. Finally, beginning with *Totem and Taboo*, Freud translates the continuity of desire through time to the level of the species. Human culture and its agent, the superego, become an endless variation upon the primal crime—upon the constitutive moment in the speciation of the human animal.

"Whether we are to attribute *reality* to unconscious wishes," Freud writes in the closing pages of the dream book, "I cannot say. It must be denied, of course, to any transitional or intermediate thoughts." Freud offers a further clarification of this curious point in the 1919 edition: "If we look at unconscious wishes reduced to their most fundamental and truest shape, we shall have to conclude, no doubt, that *psychical* reality is a particular form of existence [*Existenzform*] not to be confused with *material* reality."[18] In these formulations Freud identifies the ontological meaning of his resolution of the self into embodied desire. In finding not "transitional or intermediate thoughts" but unconscious wishes "reduced to their most fundamental and truest shape" to be a form of existence with separate status from material reality, Freud translates Descartes's antithesis of the knowing mind and the nature it knows into an opposition within nature. Unconscious wishes define a form of being that brings nature into conflict with itself. "Let us imagine ourselves," Freud suggests in "Instincts and Their Vicissitudes" (1914),

> in the situation of an almost entirely helpless living organism, as yet unoriented in the world, which is receiving stimuli in its nervous substance. This organism will very soon be in a position to make a first distinction and a first orientation. On the one hand, it will be aware of stimuli which can be avoided by muscular action (flight); these it ascribes to an external world. On the other hand, it will also be aware of stimuli against which such action is of no avail and whose character of constant pressure persists in spite of it; these stimuli are signs of an internal world, the evidence of instinctual needs. The perceptual substance of a living organism will thus have found in the efficacy of its muscular activity a basis for distinguishing between an 'outside' and an 'inside'.[19]

And a bit later in the same essay, in an examination of the "polarities" by which "our mental life as a whole is governed," Freud draws upon this biological parable in order to ground the epistemological distinction first articulated by Descartes in the rudimentary existential polarity that informs organic being.

> The antithesis ego-non-ego (external), i.e., subject-object, is, as we have already said, thrust upon the individual organism at an early stage, by the experience that it can silence *external* stimuli by means of muscular action, but is defenceless against *instinctual* stimuli. This antithesis remains, above all, sovereign in our intellectual activity and creates for research the basic situation which no efforts can alter.[20]

Thus we can see, I think, that for Freud the translation of man back into nature does not signify an alteration of the epistemological situation of understanding. Dualism remains Freud's context. What has changed with the end of metaphysics is the understanding's existential situation. Dissolving the subject's transcendent ground and enfolding the mind within nature, Darwin threw the mind back upon life as its unsurpassable reality. As a consequence, Descartes's antithesis no longer defines for Freud onto-epistemological categories grounded by reason. For the understanding that lives in the wake of Darwin's naturalization of man, the antithesis of subject and object is a fact of life as such.

PART III

THE METAMORPHOSIS
OF PSYCHOANALYTIC
THEORY

I know I am following a crooked way
in the order of my works, but it is
the order of unconscious connections.

—Freud, 1911

CHAPTER 8

The Theory of the Instincts and Its Problems

Freud's Recourse to the Language of Myth

In its final outcome, psychoanalysis fulfills the prophecy of the young Nietzsche who, in *The Birth of Tragedy*, speaks of science's "sublime metaphysical illusion"—the illusion that "thought, using the thread of logic, can penetrate the deepest recesses of being, and that thought is capable, not only of knowing being, but even of correcting it." This grand illusion "accompanies science as an instinct," with the result that "science, spurred on by its powerful illusion, speeds irresistibly to its limits where its optimism, concealed in the essence of logic, suffers shipwreck. For the periphery of the circle of science has an infinite number of points," and in their pursuit of the muse of science, men "reach . . . inevitably, such boundary points on the periphery from which one gazes into what defies illumination." The consequence of reaching the limits of what is cognitively determinable, Nietzsche tells us—and here he himself exhibits what turned out to be an oddly optimistic sensibility—is that a "new form of insight breaks through, *tragic insight*."[1] Certainly tragic insight does inform Freud's famous portrayal of the human condition in terms of the struggle of Eros and death instincts in *Civilization and Its Discontents* (1930). But more germane to our concerns here is the nature of the discourse Freud invokes to articulate that struggle. Nietzsche was prescient—or perhaps even Freud's guide—in this as well. "Myth," he tells us in these same reflections, is "the necessary consequence, indeed the purpose of science."[2]

No elaborate textual exegesis is required to demonstrate that the odyssey of psychoanalytic science finally reaches its destination through mythic discourse. In his open letter to Einstein, "Why

War?" (1932), Freud makes the point himself. At the conclusion of a long discussion on the instinctual bases of war, Freud feels impelled to justify his speculations "on an urgent practical problem" that is by nature "a concern for statesmen" and not for an "unworldly theoretician" like himself.[3] He does so in a language reminiscent of Nietzsche's. "It may perhaps seem to you as though our theories are a kind of mythology, and, in the present case, not even an agreeable one. But does not every science come in the end to a kind of mythology like this? Cannot the same be said today of your own Physics?"[4] In the *New Introductory Lectures*, composed in the same year, Freud writes in a similar vein. "The theory of the instincts is so to say our mythology. Instincts are mythical entities, magnificent in their indefiniteness. In our work we cannot for a moment disregard them, yet we are never sure we are seeing them clearly. . . . We have always been moved by a suspicion that behind all these little *ad hoc* instincts there lay concealed something serious and powerful which we should like to approach cautiously."[5]

Freud's characterization of the instincts as mythical entities, and of the theory of the instincts as a kind of mythology, is the landmark that orients the final episodes of this study. No work from Freud's pen has been held in lower esteem by his followers than the one in which the theory of the instincts is at last taken on in a comprehensive and rudimentary fashion, *Beyond the Pleasure Principle* (1920). As Ernest Jones remarks, "The book . . . is noteworthy in being the only one of Freud's which has received little acceptance on the part of his followers. Thus of the fifty or so papers that have since been directed to the topic one observes that in the first decade only half supported Freud's theory, in the second decade only a third, and in the last decade [the 1940s] none at all."[6]

A significant exception is Herbert Marcuse's *Eros and Civilization* (1955). Although Marcuse was an unorthodox adherent of the psychoanalytic outlook, his writings nonetheless stand virtually alone in according to the theory of the instincts the same paramount importance that Freud himself attached to it. Indeed, his immanent criticism of Freud's thought is itself deeply Freudian in that its purpose is to reassert the critical edge that instinct theory imparts to the psychoanalytic view of the human situation against the facile sociologism of what Marcuse calls the "neo-Freudian revisionists."[7]

Along with Marcuse, I take the theory of the instincts to be essential to Freud's thought. In this matter Freud himself is unequivocal. "The theory of the instincts," he writes in 1924, "is the most important but at the same time the least complete portion of psycho-analytic theory."[8] But I do not join Marcuse in reasserting the validity of Freud's speculations on Eros and death. Rather, my point is that we must take Freud's recourse to such speculations seriously if we are to understand in what sense the psychoanalytic venture thinks science's "instinct for truth" through to its end—how, in order to consummate the end of metaphysics on behalf of science, Freud is forced to transform his science into a mythology. Obeisance to the authority of science is what governs Freud's odyssey from beginning to end. Psychoanalysis turns to mythic discourse in pursuit of the muse of science. And while, in Freud's lifetime, science's belief that its knowledge constitutes a disclosure of nature in her objective reality was to receive a severe shock in the puzzles of quantum mechanics, the relationship of psychoanalysis to a scientific tradition whose faith in objective truth was still intact is worth recounting for what it tells us about the modern turn to psychology Freud was instrumental in defining.

A desperate and ecstatic utopianism informs Marcuse's interpretation of Freud. Nonetheless, he forces us to appreciate the fact that Freud's Eros and death instincts are not scientific concepts at all but philosophical propositions. "Freud's theory contains certain assumptions on the structure of the principal modes of being: it contains *onto*logical implications."[9] In what follows we shall see why Freud came to adopt mythic discourse in order to express what are essentially philosophic insights and why that circumstance flowed from a single-minded adherence to his original intention—that of elaborating the meaning of Darwinism for human self-understanding. We saw in part I of this study that the region of the instincts is where Freud comes face to face with his deepest and most essential insight, but we also saw that Freud was originally able to avoid posing the question of a theory of the instincts by adopting from biology a hypothesis that, in essence, handed him ready-made solutions. What interests us is that, in finally confronting and resolving the question of instinct theory on purely psychoanalytic grounds, Freud should find it necessary to adopt mythic discourse as his vehicle.

To appreciate the significance of this fact, we must first put aside the notion advanced by Ernest Jones that Freud's apparent regres-

sion to a metaphysical *Naturphilosophie* he had earlier dissociated
himself from represents the sunset thoughts of a thinker who, his scientific achievements behind him, could at last indulge a restless
speculative urge so as to find in philosophy a "goal and refuge in
. . . old age." In the end Freud does, in fact, identify psychoanalysis
with Schopenhauer's philosophy of the will.[10] But to treat Freud's
final development as a lapsing from his positivistic commitments
only obscures the fact that the summoning of mythopoeic powers in
his later years was, as Nietzsche would have it, a "necessary consequence" of his pursuit of the muse of science. Freud's theory of the
instincts represents no abandonment of Freud's commitment to sci-
ence·but rather the arrival at a mythic mode of cognition as the only
means he coud find to express a meaning that arises out of science
itself. It was precisely his pursuit of a *science* of man that brought
Freud to a boundary point on the circle of science and forced him, in
gazing beyond its periphery into what defied illumination, to realize
the impossibility of making the instinctual basis of the mind cognitively determinate *within* the discourse of science.

The Limitations of the Original Framework

To understand what is at stake in *Beyond the Pleasure Principle*,
we must come to see what brought Freud to write it in the first place.
We must ask, that is, what impelled Freud to abandon the biological
hypothesis and to place the theory of the instincts on the agenda of
psychoanalytic reflection—to do without the theoretical propping
brought to bear from without and to develop a theory of the instincts
on wholly psychoanalytic grounds. For only when his dependence
on the authority of biology turned against him did Freud discover
his need to be free of that dependence. Only then did Freud venture
to violate the constraints of dualism and decide, in *Beyond
the Pleasure Principle*, to interpret biological phenomena
psychoanalytically.

The obvious hazards of that venture enable us to sharpen the
question before us. We are now led to wonder what impelled Freud
to abandon the epistemological security of the biological hypothesis
for the philosophical adventurism of the Eros and death instincts. As
we shall see, the answer lies not in a turning back from his scientific
commitments but in a determination to pursue to ever more radical

conclusions the interpretation of man to which those commitments directed him. Ironically, Freud's adherence to those commitments both led him to discover and enabled him to surmount the limitations that the grounding operation had built into his original theoretical structure. To understand the movement from the biological hypothesis to the theory of the Eros and death instincts, we must widen the scope of our inquiry to embrace that theoretical structure as a whole.

When and how did the limitations of psychoanalytic theory appear? They appeared when Freud sought to complete his theory of the mind along the lines projected by the foundations laid down in the dream book and the *Three Essays*. "In writing," he wrote Lou Andreas-Salomé, "I have to blind myself artificially in order to focus all the light on one dark spot."[11] That is exactly what he had done in carrying out the grounding operation. Freud saw in the dreamer's withdrawal from external reality into the darkness of sleep the essential condition for the emergence of those mental manifestations that represent the unconscious primary processes of the mind— processes whose instinctual correlate is the autoerotic, and therefore equally worldless, sexual life of the infant. In both phases of the grounding operation, what, from the natural standpoint of everyday existence, appear to be the superior forces of life—the mental activities of waking consciousness and the self-preservative adaptive transactions with the external world—are subordinated and pushed into the background so as to draw the apparently inferior forces of dream consciousness and nonfunctional sexual impulses into the foreground against them.

In conformity with the theoretical experiences of Plato and Copernicus alike, Freud discovers that the power of appearances must be overcome in order to discover the reality that stands behind and grounds them. Ultimately, the mental activities of the dreamer and the neurotic afford a window into the mind's authentic reality because their mental "symptoms" appear under conditions of alienation from the realities of everyday existence. Like dreamers, "neurotics turn away from reality."[12]

In the analytic situation, hidden from the eyes and ears of the world, Freud tries to reproduce or amplify the condition of worldlessness with the technique of free association—a technique whose efficacy turns on the patient's ability to keep in abeyance the power of those internalized taboos and prohibitions that represent the adaptive necessities of his worldly commitments. In a world where science had barred the gates to metaphysics, Freud found a locus of unworldly reality in those spaces that appeared when the mind is no longer preoccupied with the business of everyday life—in the sleep of the dreamer and the withdrawal of the neurotic. These spaces he consolidated by the work of theory into the epistemic space for the disclosure of the mind's authentic being.

In turning his back on the everday world and entering into this dimension to investigate the foundations of the mind therein, Freud did not thereby simply ignore the everyday reality of life. Its presence is attested to in the negative—in dreams, as the censorship that requires unconscious impulses to take on masks and disguises, and in the sexual theory, as the developmental sequence that subordinates polymorphous perverse sexuality to the adaptive requirements of the reproductive function. In both phases of the grounding operation, Freud conceives of his task as that of penetrating beneath or reaching back behind externally imposed modifications of mental life to a more fundamental reality that is the mind's own. The theoretical operations carried out in *The Interpretation of Dreams* and the *Three Essays* proceed as reversals of the natural order of things and attest to that order by way of negation. The outlines of the completed theory project from these foundations and point in the opposite direction. To achieve that completed theory in accordance with the specifications built into its foundations, Freud has to reverse his direction once again and complete in a forward movement what he has grounded backward. Having turned his back on the external world to realize the metapsychological basis of the mind, Freud turns around once more, in the "Formulations on the Two Principles of Mental Functioning" (1911), to bring the mind's metapsychological reality back into relation with the everyday world. Taking as his starting point "the unconscious mental processes," Freud is now concerned "with the task of investigating the development of the relation of neurotics and of mankind in general to reality, and in this way of bringing the psychological significance of the real external world into the structure of our theories."[13]

The two principles of mental functioning—the reality principle and the pleasure principle—pertain most fundamentally to the two existential dimensions of organic being, that is, to the internal reality of the body, whose stimuli well up from within, and to the external reality of the environment, whose stimuli impinge upon the organism from without. "The state of psychical rest," we are told, "was originally disturbed by the peremptory demands of internal needs. When this happened, whatever was thought of (wished for) was simply presented in a hallucinatory manner, just as still happens today with our dream thoughts every night. It was only the non-occurrence of the expected satisfaction, the disappointment experienced, that led to the abandonment of this attempt at satisfaction by means of hallucination." Here the pleasure principle, manifest in the wish, displays both its power and its impotence. With the frustration of inwardly experienced need by reality, "the psychical apparatus had to decide to form a conception of the real circumstances in the external world and to endeavor to make a real alteration in them. A new principle of mental functioning was thus introduced; what was presented in the mind was no longer what was agreeable but what was real, even if it happend to be disagreeable. The setting up of the *reality principle* proved to be a momentous step."[14]

Here is where the self-preservative instinct—the side of the biological hypothesis bracketed in the *Three Essays*—is brought into play. Freud proceeds to conceptualize the activities of consciousness in terms of adaptive efficacy. "The increased significance of external reality heightened the importance, too, of the sense-organs that are directed towards the external world and of the consciousness attached to them." Consciousness is the medium for the succession of adaptations required to secure the satisfaction of internal needs in the external world, and first of all, by the institution of the "function of *attention*" and a "system of *notation*," or, in other words, of memory. In the "place of repression" consciousness develops the capacity for an "*impartial passing of judgement*." Also, "motor discharge, which, under the dominance of the pleasure principle, had served as a means of unbinding the mental apparatus of accretions of stimuli . . . by sending innervations into the interior of the body (leading to expressive movements and the play of features and to the manifestations of affect) . . . was now employed in the appropriate alteration of reality; it was converted into *action*." Finally, thinking develops as a restraint upon action, but only for the purposes of a more efficacious deployment. Thinking is "essentially an experimental kind of acting." Aside from the conscious playfulness of daydreaming and fantasying, which never mistakes itself for reality, conscious thought activity is primarily charged with the task of "reality-testing."[15]

As principles of mental functioning that denote the existential polarity of organic being, the reality and pleasure principles cut across both sides of the instinctual dualism presented by the biological hypothesis. *All* the internal needs of the infant are under the sway of the pleasure principle and its obliviousness to external reality—"a fiction," Freud comments in a long footnote, ". . . . justified when one considers that the infant—provided one includes with it the care it receives from its mother—does almost realize a psychical system of this kind." He adds, "A neat example of a psychical system shut off from the stimuli of the external world . . . is afforded by a bird's egg."[16]

Despite the fact that the two principles of mental functioning are thus more rudimentary than the instinctual dualism of the biological hypothesis, each instinct domain betrays a special affinity for one or the other of the two principles. "The supersession of the pleasure principle by the reality principle" is a development that goes on "in the ego-instincts" during which "the sexual instincts become detached from them in a very significant way. The sexual instincts behave auto-erotically at first; they obtain satisfaction in the subject's own body and therefore do not find themselves in the situation of frustration which was what necessitated the institution of the reality principle." Later on, when the "process of finding an object begins," and frustration by reality thus conditions the sexual instincts as well, "it is soon interrupted by the long period of latency."

The result of these two factors—autoeroticism and latency period—is that "the sexual instinct is held up in its psychical development and remains far longer under the dominance of the pleasure principle."[17] Indeed, this is why sexual energy is what reigns supreme in the "unconscious (repressed) processes"—processes that still remain under the dominance of the pleasure principle long after the reality principle has reshaped the activities of consciousness in accordance with the necessity to adapt to external reality. In the psychoneuroses of the adult, Freud identifies the conflict between conscious and unconscious as correlative with the conflicting tendencies of sexual and self-preservative instincts. In the functioning of the normal mind, which is the concern of the "Formulations," this conflict becomes the basis for the positive relationship between the demands of pleasure and utility.

> Just as the pleasure-ego can do nothing but *wish*, work for a yield of pleasure, and avoid unpleasure, so the reality-ego need do nothing but strive for what is *useful* and guard itself against damage. Actually the substitution of the reality principle for the pleasure principle implies no deposing of the pleasure principle, but only a safeguarding of it. A momentary pleasure, uncertain in its results, is given up, but only in order to gain along the new path an assured pleasure at a later time.[18]

With the articulation of the two principles of mental functioning, Freud's account of the mind is completed in accordance with the biological terms of reference that had underwritten the grounding operation. To be sure, the propositions set forth in the "Formulations" transcend the instinctual dualism of the biological hypothesis. The two principles reflect the existential and not the instinctual duality of organic being. The mental life of the human organism is both determined by and caught between the principles governing these two domains—the principles of pleasure and utility. Nonetheless, the two principles of mental functioning are, at bottom, extrapolations of the instinctual duality. For without the sexual instinct as the biological ground of possibility for the continued dominance of the pleasure principle in the processes of the unconscious, the domain of pleasure would long ago have been absorbed into the adaptive instrumentalism that marks the sway of the reality principle in the processes of consciousness.

It is exactly here, however, on the side of the human organism's self-preservative adaptations to reality, that Freud's use of the biological hypothesis to underwrite his theoretical structure wreaks its revenge. In its utterly utilitarian and necessity-bound adaptive transactions with the external world, the self-preservative instinct offers no surplus of instinctual energy. Yet instinct theory requires just such a surplus if it is to account for that dimension of the individual's relations with the external world that stands beyond the rigors of adaptive necessity—the domain of cultural meanings that structure human reality and distinguish the human animal from amongst the creatures of nature. Since, for Freud, all meaning is in principle psychogenic, the cultural life-world must also have an instinctual basis. And in the *Three Essays* Freud had already fixed on the interruption of human sexual development by the latency period as "one of the necessary conditions of the aptitude of men for developing a higher civilization, but also for their tendency to neurosis."[19]

In 1910, when the realm of cultural meaning had already begun to become a focus of interest, Freud made explicit his intention to deploy sexuality as the ground of possibility for these manifestations of mind as well. "The light thrown by psychology on the evolution of our civilization [Kultur]," he announced somewhat prematurely, "has shown that it originates mostly at the cost of the sexual component instincts, and that these must be suppressed, restricted, transformed and directed to higher aims, in order that the mental constructions of civilization may be established."[20] To pursue the vicissitudes of erotic desire into the external world in the construction of a cultural life-world, however, Freud would need an instinct theory that transcended the determinations of the biological hypothesis. For how could there even *be* a world for a self whose relations with external reality were energized by the instinct for self-preservation and defined by utility and necessity? Even where the human animal is engaged in attending to its life needs, it still find itself moving within a world of significations and not merely a natural environment. As Marx was anxious to point out, even the utilitarian transactions of the marketplace involve an exchange of man-created values. With Freud's completion of his theory of the mind in accordance with its original specifications, he reached an impasse that prevented him from making sense of the world in which human existence lives its reality—of the shared world of meaning to which every human utterance in one way or another attests. Let us see how he surmounted that obstacle and with what consequences.

CHAPTER 9

From the Science of Meaning
to the Meaning of Science

The Leap into the Anthropological Dimension

As soon as Freud attempts to draw the psychological significance of external reality into the structure of psychoanalytic theory, the biological terms of reference underwriting it become explicit and expose a serious difficulty. Freud can bring external reality into his theory only at the rudimentary level of the relation between the organism and the environment. In this way the reality principle at least serves to clarify the limitations of Freud's original theoretical structure by providing a measure of the distance between the merely organic and the specifically human experience of external reality. The "Formulations" thus prepared the way for Freud's leap into the dimension that denotes the specifically human relation to external reality. But, as we shall see, the reality principle also serves a positive function in establishing the new turn of understanding that begins in *Totem and Taboo*. The insights of Herbert Marcuse will help us see how.

In *Eros and Civilization* (1955) Herbert Marcuse seizes on the biologism that informs the reality principle as his point of leverage for transforming the theory of repression, articulated by Freud as the biological fate of the human animal, into a critical theory of repressive civilization—a dialectical sublation of Freudian theory that enables Marcuse to present the vision of a nonrepressive civilization as the possible historical future of mankind. Marcuse's argument, however, will serve here a very different purpose. It directs us unwittingly, as it were, to the sublation by which Freud himself surmounts the limitations of his original theoretical structure and initiates the dialectical adventure that follows in the wake of *Totem and Taboo*. "The reality principle," Marcuse begins, sustains the organism in the external world. In the case of the human organism, this is an historical world . . . . It has been argued that Freud's concept of the *reality principle* obliterates this fact by making historical contingencies into biological necessities: his analysis of the repressive transformations of the instincts under the impact of the reality principle generalizes from a specific historical form of reality to reality pure and simple.[1]

Marcuse grants the validity of this argument, not in order to join critics in refuting psychoanalytic theory, but in order to gain leverage for an immanent critique aimed at elevating that theory to a level not subject to the same attack. The validity of the charge of biologism, we read, "does not vitiate the truth in Freud's generalization, namely, that a repressive organization of the instincts underlies *all* historical forms of the reality principle in civilization. . . . Precisely because all civilization has been organized domination, the historical development assumes the dignity and necessity of a universal biological development."[2] Thus, in order to recapture this truth from its positivistic falsification, Marcuse proposes that we unfold the "historical substance" of Freud's insights, which appear in Freud's theoretical propositions "only in a reified form as natural (biological) processes."[3] Marcuse proceeds to do this by way of an "extrapolation"—a "duplication of concepts" in which Freud's biological terms of reference are "paired with corresponding terms denoting the specific socio-historic component."[4] At this point Marcuse introduces the concepts that are central to his dialectical critique and sublation of psychoanalytic theory—namely, "*Surplus-repression:* the restrictions necessitated by social domination" and the "*Performance principle:* the prevailing form the the *reality principle.*"[5]

Marcuse sheds an important light on the limitations of Freud's early theory.[6] What he fails to come to grips with, however, is the fact that in the "Formulations," where the reality principle is first articulated, Freud himself advances some propositions that already recapture the sociohistorical dimension which the reality principle reifies at the level of biological necessity.

The "endopsychic impression" made by the substitution of the reality principle for the pleasure principle, Freud tells us, "has been so powerful that it is reflected in a special religious myth. The doctrine of reward in the afterlife for the—voluntary or enforced—renunciation of earthly pleasures is nothing other than a mythical projection of this revolution in the mind."[7] Here, the transformation of metaphysics into metapsychology, heralded ten years earlier in *The Psychopathology of Everyday Life,* achieves its first rudimentary and concrete determination. The religious vision of another world, a world of true being, a preeminently metaphysical world, is disclosed here to be a projection of psychical factors and relations of the mind—namely, the subordination of the primary processes under the dominion of the pleasure principle into the unconscious as a result of the mind's accession to the demands of reality. Religion acknowledges the power of those demands by disavowing them, by subordinating the privations imposed by biological necessity once again to the prospective gratifications of a superior world.

In this projection, however, religion marks not the supersession of the pleasure principle by the reality principle but the sublation of the pleasure principle to the level of metaphysical meaning—of meaning that is understood to lie behind the appearances of the world as their transcendental ground. Freud continues, "religions have been able to effect absolute renunciation of pleasure in this life by means of the promise of compensation in a future existence; *but they have not by this means achieved a conquest of the pleasure principle* [my italics]. It is *science* that comes nearest to succeeding in that conquest."[8] In the assertion that *science* "comes nearest to" the conquest of the pleasure principle by the reality principle, while religions represent what are obviously *historical* forms of the pleasure principle, Freud enters emphatically into the anthropological dimension—into the domain of shared cultural meanings in which the evidences of man *qua* man subsist. That is, Freud recapitulates a fundamentally biological event in the ontogeny of the individual as a historical event in the life of the human species. Religions represent the collective mental projections of a mankind that has not yet come to grips with the reality of the world through science. They are historical manifestations of mind under the sway of the pleasure principle. Science is that acquisition of the human species by which the reality principle comes consciously into force. By implication, psychoanalytic science is itself the consummation of that consciousness for the species.

Now, against Freud's extrapolation of the reality principle into the sociohistorical dimension, Marcuse could legitimately reassert his original criticism of Freud's biologism. For Freud's extrapolation to the level of historical meaning cannot be carried out within the biologistic terms of reference that govern the articulation of the two principles of mental functioning. We already know why Freud's extrapolation is epistemologically unjustifiable. The adaptive necessities that structure the activities of consciousness under the sway of the reality principle are clearly articulated on the biological model of organism-environment. External reality is here at once indeterminate and implacable in the sheer positivity of its objects—objects that have no meaning for the organism aside from their utility or nonutility for the satisfaction of its bodily needs. This "real external world" is not and cannot be made to represent a human life-world. But Marcuse's original criticism—or rather the undiminished cogency of his original criticism—only helps us to see why Freud's epistemologically questionable recapitulation of biological necessity at the level of historical meaning marks the turning point in his thought—a turning point whose ultimate consequence is the radical reconceptualization of his theory of the mind. In the assertion that science is the historical realization of the reality principle for the human species, Freud is no longer operating within the theoretical framework laid down in the grounding operation and brought to completion in the "Formulations." He has leapt beyond the biological confines of that framework into the domain of worldly meaning.

This leap beyond the domain of biological necessity into the domain of worldly meaning, heralded by the "Formulations," is completed in *Totem and Taboo,* where Freud fixes on social reality as the context for the psychoanalytic investigation of the "mental constructions of civilization."

> The asocial nature of the neuroses has its genetic origin in their most fundamental purpose, which is to take flight from an unsatisfying reality into a more pleasurable world of phantasy. *The real world, which is avoided in this way by neurotics, is under the sway of human society and of the institutions collectively created by it.* To turn away from reality is at the same time to withdraw from the community of man. [my italics][9]

Here Freud explicitly identifies the "real world," not with an indeterminate biological environment, but with the collective reality of human society and its institutions. The question this identification poses is this: if the framework of Freud's original theory effaces the dimension of the human life-world, how does it become the epistemic domain for the psychoanalytic investigation of civilization in *Totem and Taboo*?

The radical reconceptualization of Freud's theory of the mind, which culminates in *The Ego and the Id* with a psychology of the ego and its dependent relations, arises out of Freud's leap from the level of biological necessity to the level of cultural meaning—a leap heralded in the "Formulations" and accomplished definitively in *Totem and Taboo*. The two major aspects in the development of that later theory may be cited here to indicate its relation to the anthropological heights attained in *Totem and Taboo*. First, there is the transposition of the locus of psychical reality from the unconscious to the ego, from wishing to willing—a transposition that reflects Freud's belated recognition that the mind *lives* its meaning in the *world* and not in the worldless depths of the unconscious. Second, and concomitantly, the theory of the instincts is placed on the agenda of psychoanalytic theory with the realization that the biological hypothesis makes survival the sum and substance of the individual's transactions with reality and is therefore unable to serve as the instinctual basis for meaning lived in the world through the products of culture.

The two major aspects of Freud's later development sharpen our understanding of how, given the biologistic confines of his original theory, Freud is able to get a fix on the domain of culture in *Totem and Taboo*. The key to our answer lies in the fact that, despite the metamorphosis of psychoanalytic theory, whose whole purpose is to overcome the theory's original limitations, Freud never altered or abandoned the reality principle, in whose very formulation those limitations became patent. The reason Freud never abandoned the reality principle, I think, is not hard to discern. Freud's positivistic commitments assured him that, in essence, man was a product of nature. Consequently the "mental apparatus," as he preferred to call it, must have a biological raison d'être which could only be that of facilitating the gratification of instinctual needs in the external world. The reality principle was the mark of Freud's unequivocal commitment to the certainty of science in the truth of its own knowledge, and thus served to guarantee Freud's own certainty in the scientific integrity of his endeavor.

In the very biological necessity that informs the reality principle, psychoanalysis basks in the light of science's self-certainty that man is descended from nature. In leaping beyond the realm of biological necessity into the domain of worldly meaning, Freud does not for a moment abandon the security afforded him by this self-certainty. On the contrary, that scientific self-certainty, marked in Freud's thought by the reality principle, is itself the means by which Freud plants himself down and orients psychoanalytic vision within man's cultural world—the world whose metapsychological basis *Totem and Taboo* undertakes to disclose. In *positing* the advent of science as the historical appearance of the reality principle for the species, Freud does not thereby treat the cultural realization of the reality principle as a historical contingency. Instead, he elevates biological necessity, represented in the reality principle's conquest of the pleasure principle, into the life world, where it appears as the historical meaning of science.

The extrapolation of science's self-certainty from the level of biological necessity to the level of historical meaning is what enables Freud to raise his theoretical vision from the worldless depths of the unconscious beyond the utilitarian domain of self-preservation to a world lived beyond biological necessity in the meanings of culture, and to find a ground of certainty therein. Freud thus stakes his whole interpretation of culture on the self-certainty of science that its cognitive achievements represent the authoritative disclosure of nature's reality. As the reality principle of the species, science represents the self-evident criterion of truth in confronting the manifestations of mind that structure the sociohistorical dimension of human life. Freud's faith in the power of science to disclose truth guards him against the hazards of historicism that plagued Dilthey's ventures into this same realm—a realm Dilthey called "objective mind." As Freud wrote James Putnam in 1915, "I have never been concerned with any comprehensive synthesis, but invariably with certainty alone. And it is worth sacrificing everything to the latter."[10]

As a positivist surveying the landscape of cultural meaning, Freud could be certain of only one thing, that science had stripped the veil of religion from the life world by exposing men to the stark reality of their fortuitous appearance within the existent. From this ground of certainty, secured in science's self-certainty, proceeds the whole psychoanalytic interpretation of the evolution of culture in *Totem and Taboo*. The identification of the historical appearance of science with the biological event marked by the supersession of the pleasure principle in the ontogeny of the mind is what structures the account of man's cultural evolution in the third essay of *Totem and Taboo*.

In accordance with the biogenetic law, whose logic, as we saw, already informs Freud's account of individual psychogenesis, man's phylogenetic travail marks out the path that, for the individual, ontogeny recapitulates. After arguing that the earliest "animistic" *Weltanschauung* of the human species is characterized by a belief in the "omnipotence of thoughts," Freud advances the following propositions:

> If we are prepared to accept this account . . . of the evolution of human views of the universe—an animistic phase followed by a religious phase and this in turn by a scientific one—it will not be difficult to follow the vicissitudes of the 'omnipotence of thoughts' through these different phases. At the animistic phase men ascribe omnipotence to *themselves*. At the religious stage they transfer it to the gods but do not seriously abandon it themselves, for they reserve the power of influencing the gods in a variety of ways in accordance to their wishes. The scientific view of the universe no longer affords any room for human omnipotence; men have acknowledged their smallness and submitted resignedly to death and to the other necessities of nature. None the less some of the primitive belief in omnipotence still survives in men's faith in the power of the human mind, which grapples with the laws of reality.[11]

Freud's certainty that in the scientific age the mind grapples with the "laws of reality" reaffirms the identification he made in the "Formulations" between science and the reality principle.

An Amplification

Freud's account of the "evolution of human views of the universe" needs some amplification if we are to understand how science can represent the reality principle for the species. We find this further amplification in the *New Introductory Lectures* (1933) where Freud, in his putatively Romantic period, both clarifies and strengthens his positivistic account of man's cultural evolution by arguing that science itself is *not* a *Weltanschauung*. In this, Freud attempts to move to safer ground, since a world-view necessarily signifies a perspective on the world gained from the standpoint of an idea. And, as opposed to "reality," a mere idea, however deeply rooted or pervasive, is by nature historically surpassable. Thus in denying science the dubious honor of constituting a world view, Freud actually seeks to shelter science, and its meaning in the evolution of culture, from the winds of historicism.

A *"Weltanschaunng,"* we are told, "is an intellectual construction which solves all the problems of existence uniformly on the basis of one overriding hypothesis, which, accordingly, leaves no question unanswered and in which everything that interests us finds its fixed place." Now psychoanalysis, as a *science* of the mind,

> is quite unable to construct a *Weltanschauung* of its own: it must accept the scientific one. *But the Weltanschauung of science already departs notably from our definition* [my italics]. It is true that it too assumes the *uniformity* of the explanation of the universe; but it does so only as a programme, the fulfilment of which is relegated to the future. Apart from this it is marked by negative characteristics, by its limitation to what is at the moment knowable and by its sharp rejection of certain elements that are alien to it.[12]

Freud then proceeds to identify, in informal terms, the cognitive activities of science with the activities of consciousness under the sway of the reality principle, but now with some arresting distinctions.

> Scientific thinking does not differ in its nature from the normal activity of thought, which all of us . . . employ in looking after our affairs in ordinary life. It has only developed certain features: it takes an interest in things even if they have no immediate tangible use; it is careful to avoid individual factors and affective influences; it examines strictly the trust-worthiness of the sense-perceptions on which it bases its conclusions; it provides itself with new perceptions which cannot be obtained by everyday means and it isolates the determinates of these new experiences in experiments which are deliberately varied. It endeavours to arrive at correspondence with reality—that is to say, with what exists outside us and independently of us, and as experience has taught us, is decisive for the fulfilment or disappointment of our wishes. This correspondence with the real external world we call 'truth'. It remains the aim of scientific work even if we leave the practical value of that work out of account.[13]

These wholly orthodox expressions of Enlightenment science's self-understanding clarify for us why science represents for Freud the reality principle of the species. Science is not an all-embracing world view premised on one overriding idea, but a development of that everyday utilitarianism in which we again see the image of adaptive necessity.

But Freud's amplifications also raise a new question, the answer to which already lies in *Totem and Taboo* and brings us to a deeper understanding of its logic. The question is this: if the thought activity of science is conducted in an epistemic space purified of utilitarian interest in things, of individual factors and affective influences, and constitutes its phenomena within that space by systematically doubting appearances and obtaining for itself new perceptions unavailable by everyday means, and if science adopts this objective standpoint for the sake of securing the truth of its cognitions in a correspondence with the reality that exists *outside* and *independently* of us, how is it possible for science to appear *within* the human lifeworld to which the standpoint of science is opposed?

The answer is that the meaning of science has appeared, not through the abstract theoretical achievements of Copernicus, Newton, or Darwin, but by virtue of the potentiality that inheres in science's way of apprehending and comprehending the data of the existent—that is, in experimentalism, whose significance for the life world was forecast by Bacon in his famous equation of knowledge and power. The meaning of science has appeared for the world in technology. Not science itself but its practical efficacy as the way to a new and powerful art of making is what, in radically altering the conditions of everyday existence, has enabled science to appear in the domain of worldly reality.

In an essay on "The Claims of Psychoanalysis to Scientific Interest" (1913), written shortly after the completion of *Totem and Taboo,* Freud restates the phylogenetic account of the third Essay, but this time from the standpoint, not of science as such, but of technology.

An investigation of primitive peoples shows mankind caught up to begin with in a childish belief in its own omnipotence. A whole number of mental structures can thus be understood as attempts to deny whatever might disturb this feeling of omnipotence and so *to prevent emotional life from being affected by reality until the latter could be better controlled and used for purposes of satisfaction.* The principle of avoiding unpleasure dominates human actions until it is replaced by the better one of *adaptation to the external world. Pari passu* with men's *progressive control over the world* goes a development in their *Weltanschauung,* their view of the universe as a whole. They turn away more and more from their original belief in their own omnipotence rising from an animistic phase through a religious to a scientific one. [my italics][14]

In these formulations Freud anticipates the understanding of that modern heir to Comte's positive philosophy, system theory, for which science is the organ of man's instrumental adaptation to nature.[15]

The Introduction of Narcissism

The amplification of how, for Freud, science stands as the reality principle of the species has been a digression from our central concern. As the scientific analysis of man's mythico-religious illusions, *Totem and Taboo* deals primarily with the fate of the pleasure principle, from which those illusions have sprung. At the same time, our digression has been a necessary one. It has shown us how, by securing his ground of certainty in science's self-certainty of its hold on reality, Freud is able to make good the elevation of the reality principle from the level of biological necessity to the level of historical meaning. Science *is* the historical manifestation of the reality principle. By the same token, religion is the historical manifestation of the pleasure principle. In order to show the metapsychological basis of man's metaphysical illusions, Freud also had to elevate the pleasure principle to the level of historical meaning. And, in this case, that meant conceptualizing the activities of libido such that they could become manifest as the historical vicissitudes of desire arising out of relations of self and world.

To afford this possibility to libido, Freud had to make a decisive modification of his ontogenetic account of the psyche. It is here that the internal dialectic of Freud's thought, initiated by his return to the world and elevation of the reality principle into the domain of historical meaning, secures the ground from which the theory of the Eros and death instincts arises.

This modification in the theory of psychosexual development takes place in *Totem and Taboo* at the point where Freud draws out the ontogenetic recapitulation on which his phylogenetic account is modeled.

If we may regard the existence among primitive races of the omnipotence of thoughts as evidence in favor of narcissism, we are encouraged to attempt a comparison between the phases in the development of men's view of the universe and the stages of an individual's libidinal development. The animistic phase would correspond to narcissism both chronologically and in its content; the religious phase would correspond to the stage of object-choice of which the characteristic is a child's attachment to his parents; while the scientific phase would have an exact counterpart in the stage at which an individual has reached maturity, has renounced the pleasure principle, adjusted himself to reality and turned to the external world for the object of his desires.[16]

Now, at the ontogenetic level, Freud had previously identified the starting point of libidinal development with autoeroticism—with the pleasure the various organs of the body take in their own functioning. In *Totem and Taboo,* however, something new is introduced into ontogeny.[17] Now it is no longer autoeroticism but narcissism that is designated as the starting point. *Totem and Taboo* prepares the reader for this change by preceding the comparison of ontogeny and phylogeny by a new account of the stages of libidinal development—an account that explicitly introduces narcissism into the developmental sequence.

Freud starts by summarizing the account already established in the *Three Essays* whereby the sexual instincts are initially autoerotic. "The separate instinctual components of sexuality work independently of one another to obtain pleasure and find satisfaction in the subject's own body." This stage "is succeeded by one in which an object is chosen." At this point, however, Freud introduces something new into his schema. He now finds that "it is expedient and indeed indispensable to insert" an intermediate stage into this account—a stage at which "the hitherto isolated sexual instincts have already come together into a single whole and have also found an object. But this object is not an external one, extraneous to the subject, but its own ego, which has been constituted at about this same time." This stage, which he calls narcissism, is marked by the fact that "the subject behaves as if he were in love with himself."[18]

Why does Freud find it "expedient and indeed indispensable" to introduce this new stage into the libidinal development of the individual? Most fundamentally, narcissism was necessitated, not in the first place by ontogenetic considerations, but in order to make possible the interpretation of the phenomena of culture as "external" manifestations of mind under the sway of the pleasure principle. Indeed, this is indicated rather obviously by the fact that when *Totem and Taboo* comes around to comparing ontogeny with phylogeny, the autoerotic phase drops out of the picture altogether. In fact, the more deeply Freud becomes committed to the life world as the scene of action where mind has its substantive reality, the more fundamental narcissism becomes within psychoanalytic theory, until finally, in its later articulations, narcissism comes to signify the self-sufficiency of the instincts during the intrauterine existence that precedes the irruption of the self into the world.

How is it then that the introduction of narcissism solved the problem of elevating the pleasure principle into the domain of worldly meaning? The historical manifestations of mind under the sway of the pleasure principle confronted Freud, let us remember, with the presence of meanings that subsist in the relations of self and world. Since the whole effort of psychoanalysis is to disclose the instinctual provenance of meaning, the meanings of culture also had to be treated as the manifestations of unconscious desire. That is, the instinctual strivings for gratification had to be afforded the possibility of materializing in the world to be experienced as meaning that arises from without.

In the story of Narcissus's rapture in the contemplation of his own image, Freud found the perfect representation of this possibility as one inherent to desire itself. What desire desires, as Hegel once put it, is *itself*. Narcissism represents the situation in which desire finds gratification in the experience of its own image. The narcissist thinks the world *of* himself and takes himself *for* the world. Autoeroticism, on the other hand, is *worldless* and refers us to the pleasure functioning of the body. Narcissism transcends the purely organic manifestations of desire by directing us to desire's constitution of a world that is not affected by reality. Narcissism thus provides the needed ontogenetic basis for the phylogenetic manifestations of mind under the sway of the pleasure principle—of mind that lives in a world but is as yet unaffected by the naked positivity of reality that science discloses to be the objective state of things. Thus the animistic phase of the mind's phylogeny is characterized by the "omnipotence of thoughts."

> The first picture which men formed of the world—animism—was a *psychological* one. It needed no scientific basis as yet, since science only begins after it has been realized that the world is unknown, and that means must therefore be sought for getting to know it. . . . [Primitive man] knew what things were like in the world, namely just as he

felt himself to be. . . . He turns his emotional cathexes into persons, he peoples the world with them and meets his internal mental processes outside himself again. [my italics][19]

Into this scheme, then, religion fits as a halfway point between the unfettered sway of the pleasure principle and the ascendance of the reality principle. Religion, that is, reflects the institution of repression. In the religious vision of another world—a higher reality that stands beyond the appearances of the everyday world—the pleasure principle is displaced from the worldly domain it occupies under animism. In religion, the pleasure principle still holds sway, but now in an emphatically metaphysical realm. Animism thus represents a more primordial configuration of "objective mind" than does religion. In *Totem and Taboo* it serves to open the psychoanalytic perspective onto the worldly scene of action in which the drama of the primal crime is enacted in the fourth essay as the species-constitutive institution of repression. Finally, science represents the last stage of mankind's coming to grips with the real external world. Science substitutes for animism's psychological picture of the world the metapsychological one psychoanalysis consummates.

CHAPTER 10

The Philosophy of Desire

The introduction of the concept of narcissism was prompted by the theoretical needs of Freud's interpretation of culture. The scene of action where the mental constructions of civilization arise is in the nexus of meaningful relations that subsists between self and world. The concept of narcissism makes it possible to conceive of these relations as instinctual in origin—as springing from something inherent to libido.

As soon as Freud had completed the final essay of *Totem and Taboo*, he returned to the level of individual psychology to write "On Narcissism: An Introduction" (1914). The formal introduction of the concept of narcissism into psychoanalytic theory, "On Narcissism" marks the starting point of the cycle of developments culminating in the radical reconceptualization of that theory. The continuity between Freud's early and late theory of the mind is not that of a smooth development or completion. The cycle of developments initiated by the introduction of narcissism defines an authentically dialectical movement.

In the course of this movement, psychoanalytic theory is founded for a second time, but now at a new existential level. The psychoanalytic perspective is displaced upward and focused on the relations of self and world. Freud abandons the systematic, substantive sense of the unconscious and transposes the locus of psychical reality to an ego that subsists in a nexus of dependent relations with the id, the superego, and external reality.

In this second foundation a new grounding operation is carried out as a reversal of the first. Freud begins at the lower, instinctual

130

level in *Beyond the Pleasure Principle* (1920) and finishes at the higher, psychological level in *The Ego and the Id* (1923). *The Ego and the Id* closes the cycle when, with the concept of the superego, Freud forges the link between the anthropology of *Totem and Taboo* and the psychology that flows from it. If, in Freud's original theory, the body in its impulsive welling up from within denotes the mind's ultimate ground, the superego serves the same function at the new level Freud's theory operates at. Standing "between" the ego and the id, the superego denotes the constitutional basis of the psyche, the phylogenetically acquired "archaic heritage" of mankind's passage out of the state of nature. Nature now stands fixed at the core of the mind as the remnant of an event in the natural history of the species—an event that marks the institution of repression for the species and implicates the human animal irrevocably in a world of shared cultural meaning. At the same time, the living nature within which man is thus differentiated is now construed philosophically in terms of the struggle of the Eros and death instincts. Freud's science turns into a mythology. The meaning of Darwinism for human self-understanding comes to its final expression in a philosophy of desire. Our task in this chapter is to elucidate the logic by which that philosophy unfolds, to chart the path traversed from the introduction of the concept of narcissism to the articulation of the theory of the Eros and death instincts.

In "On Narcissism" Freud refocuses libido theory at the level of the relations of self and world. The concept of narcissism consists in "the idea of there being an original libidinal cathexis of the ego, from which some is later given off to objects, but which fundamentally persists and is related to the object-cathexes much as the body of an amoeba is related to the pseudopodia it puts out."[1]

Freud's use of the metaphor of the amoeba to characterize the activities of libido actually inverts the picture we are given of the instinctual energies in its earlier articulations. In that earlier picture, sexuality dwells in the lower layer of the mind, in the unconscious, while the self-preservative instincts, operating at the level of consciousness, stand face to face with the external world. Now, "as regards the differentiation of psychical energies, we are led to the conclusion that to begin with, during the state of narcissism, they exist together; not until there is object-cathexis is it possible to discrimi-

nate a sexual energy—libido—from an energy of the ego-instincts."[2]
Here libido is manifest in the external relations of the self with a
world of loved objects, while the ego instincts remain centered on
the self and its survival activities.

But Freud was quick to see that the idea of an original libidinal
cathexis of the "ego" (which here means only the organism as a totality) obliterates the significance of the biological distinction between sexuality and self-preservation for psychoanalytic theory.
Self-preservation could easily enough be construed narcissistically
as the organism's desire to keep itself in being. Narcissistic libido
then raised the possibility of postulating "a single kind of psychical
energy."[3] But to do so would mean abadoning the vital connection
with biological science, which had formerly underwritten Freud's
whole theoretical enterprise.

In this context Freud expresses the need for a "theory of the instincts which would help us find our bearings,"[4] and makes explicit
for the first time the fact that the instinct hypothesis, which he had to
this point been working with, was not based on psychoanalytic insight but "derives its principal support from biology."[5]

"On Narcissism" merely places the theory of the instincts on
Freud's theoretical agenda without pursuing it. Nonetheless, his
discussion of the problem of instinct theory ends with a clear indi-
cation of how he intended to proceed: "Since we cannot wait for another science to present us with final conclusions on the theory of
the instincts, it is far more to our purpose that we should try to see
what light may be thrown upon this basic problem of biology by a
synthesis of *psychological* phenomena."[6]

However modestly stated, this proposal marks a rudimentary reversal of method. At the beginning of the psychoanalytic venture
Freud had turned to biological science for guidance, for an objective
guidepost toward which to orient his investigations of the dark
depths of human subjectivity. Now, having for purely psychoanalytic reasons extended libido to the point of effacing the biological distinction that had originally secured his foothold in the domain of organic reality, Freud contemplates addressing this "basic problem of
biology" by a synthesis of psychological phenomena—that is, *on
psychoanalytic grounds alone.* In this reversal the possibility, or
even the necessity, of interpreting biological phenomena psychoan-

alytically arises. *Beyond the Pleasure Principle* is a measure of the radicalism with which Freud pursued that possibility.[7]

None of Freud's works is so tortuously argued as *Beyond the Pleasure Principle*. The argument, he cautions the reader, "is speculation, often far-fetched speculation . . . an attempt to follow out an idea consistently to see where it will lead."[8] This disclaimer, however, did not prevent Freud from making the results of these speculations central to his final theory of the mind. What it attests to is Freud's awareness that he was traversing hazardous territory.

What seems to have troubled Freud most of all is that *Beyond the Pleasure Principle* forfeited the security of those epistemological constraints he to this point had so scrupulously respected.

> It should be made quite clear that the uncertainty of our speculation has been greatly increased by the necessity of borrowing from the science of biology. Biology is truly the land of unlimited possibilities. We may expect it to give us the most surprising information and we cannot guess what answers it will return in a few dozen years to the questions we have put to it. They may be of a kind which will blow away the whole of our artificial structure of hypotheses.[9]

Yet this statement should not be read to mean that Freud *derives* his theory of the Eros and death instincts from biology. Rather, his concern with biological research and findings is twofold. First, he is concerned that his hypothesis of a death instinct not have some biological reason for being ruled out of order. "Thus," he notes after an extended consideration of the biological treatment of death, "our expectation that biology would flatly contradict the recognition of the death instincts has not been fulfilled. We are at liberty to continue concerning ourselves with their possibility, if we have other reasons for doing so."[10] Second, and more radically, Freud turns to biology for phenomena that he uses psychoanalytic insight to explain. The Eros instincts are developed by the application of "the libido theory which has been arrived at in psycho-analysis to the mutual relationship of cells."[11]

Not surprisingly, the libido theory that Freud applies to the mutual relationship of cells is nothing other than narcissism. "With the hypothesis of narcissistic libido and the extension of the concept of libido to the individual cells, the sexual instinct was transformed for us into Eros, which seeks to force together and hold together portions of living substance," he explains in a long footnote on the development of his views on the instincts.

> What are commonly called the sexual instincts are looked upon by us as the part of Eros which is directed towards objects. Our speculations have suggested that Eros operates from the beginning of life and appears as a "life instinct" in opposition to the "death instinct" which was brought into being by the coming to life of inorganic substance. These speculations seek to solve the riddle of life by supposing that these two instincts were struggling with each other from the first.[12]

Clearly, these propositions are baldly vitalistic, and, as such, they place the adherents of the psychoanalytic tradition in an embarrassing position with respect to the scientific claims of its founder. This embarrassment is understandable but also, I think, misplaced. For the theory of the instincts is the authentic outcome of Freud's adherence to the truths science had disclosed through Darwin. Before suggesting what I think we should make of this outcome, the philosophical purport of Freud's theory must be clarified.

Freud begins his consideration of the instincts first by establishing the death instinct in the proposition that *"an instinct is an urge in organic life to restore an earlier state of things."*[13] On this view, "the phenomena of organic development must be attributed to external disturbing and diverting influences," which oblige the organism "to diverge ever more widely from its original course of life and to make ever more complicated detours before reaching its aim of death."[14] It is only after the establishment of the death instincts that, by an extension of libido theory, Freud introduces the life instincts at the level of individual cells. Abandoning their original narcissism, individual cells take each other as love objects and "partly neutralize the death instincts. . . in those cells and thus preserve their life."[15] The "life process of the individual leads for internal reasons to an abolition of chemical tensions, that is to say, death, whereas union with the living substance of a different individual increases those tensions, introducing what may be described as fresh 'vital differences' which must then be lived off."[16] Thus, with the introduction of Eros, the disturbing influences that divert the death instinct from achieving its goal of extinguishing all the tensions of life are identified, though not exclusively, with other living organisms.

Now the role of narcissism in the conceptualization of the Eros instincts is obvious. What is not obvious is that narcissism also pointed the way to the death instincts. In fact, Freud develops his theory of the instincts as a whole by way of a reflection on the meaning of desire implicit in his theory of narcissism and its manifestations. The embodiment of that meaning in a theory of the Eros and death instincts makes the theory philosophical because the instincts now *encompass* rather than merely subtend the relations between self and world in which human life has its reality. In the theory of the Eros and death instincts, that is, biology is made directly meaningful for life in a way that scientific cognition can never be.

We saw that Freud introduced narcissism as a fundamental stage of libidinal development in order to gain access to the domain of cultural phenomena. Preparatory to the task of *Totem and Taboo,* and in conjunction with the composition of the "Formulations," Freud in 1910 undertook for the first time to analyze paranoia—the pathology of projected meaning par excellence—in "Psycho-analytic Notes on an Autobiographical Account of a Case of Paranoia *(Dementia Paranoides),*" or, for short, the Schreber case. In 1901 Freud had already cited paranoia as the analogy for understanding the projection of psychology into the external world in the construction of a supernatural reality. Only when the task of interpreting culture was fixed on his mental horizon did Freud finally take on the analysis of paranoia, however.[17] And here, in a strictly clinical context—or pseudoclinical context, since the Schreber case is based on an autobiographical account of the illness—Freud first tries out the notion of narcissism, without yet committing himself to its place within psychoanalytic theory.

Crucial to Freud's analysis of Schreber's paranoia is the proposition that *"the delusional formation, which we take to be the pathological product, is in reality an attempt at recovery, a process of reconstruction."*[18] The fully pathological aspect of paranoia is the state of narcissistic withdrawal from the world—the "repression" of the relations of self and world that precedes the manifestation of paranoiac symptoms. This state of withdrawal "happens silently; we receive no intelligence of it, but can only infer it from subsequent events. What forces itself so noisily upon our attention is the process of recovery, which undoes the work of repression and brings back libido again onto the people it had abandoned."[19]

Striking in Freud's analysis is the contrast he draws between the delusional projections of the paranoiac and the symptoms of hysteria, the central clinical model of repressed, rather than projected, unconscious meaning. "Paranoia decomposes just as hysteria condenses. Or rather, paranoia resolves once more into their elements the products of the condensations and identifications which are effected in the unconscious."[20] The hysterical symptom, that is, represents a condensation that the work of interpretation resolves once more into the network of meanings structuring the unconscious. Paranoia, on the other hand, scatters the contents of the unconscious into the world, where they are experienced by the paranoiac as meaning materialized from without. In his most radical expression of this phenomenon, Freud abandons the idea that projection is the proper way to characterize it. "It was incorrect to say that the perception which was suppressed internally is projected outwards," he tells us in the closing pages of the Schreber case, "the truth is rather, we can now see, what was abolished internally returns from without."[21]

Now the quiescent state of narcissistic withdrawal, inferred from the subsequent noisy manifestations of meaning that appear from without, signifies something that already transcends Freud's original theory of the mind. It signifies an *unconscious self*. In the state of unconscious self-absorption, desire takes itself for the world, thus denoting in libidinal terms the possibility of a self that has a world. In taking itself *for* the world, however, the narcissistic self is at once oblivious to the external world and unconscious of itself. For narcissistic withdrawal gains its quiescence from the fact that, when in a state of self-possession, desire extinguishes desire. The gratification of desire is at once its abolition. It is only by its irruption into the world that libido once again becomes manifest as striving, as a longing for itself in which desire seeks to overcome its loss of self-possession by materializing outside of itself its object of desire, and finding gratification therein. The materializations of desire in the external world arise from the disturbance of desire's self-possession, in which the state of being everything for itself is also a pure nothingness—an unconscious self. In the concept of narcissism, libido is uprooted from its identification with the biological function of sexuality and becomes conceptually self-sustaining. No longer dependent on biological science, libido theory is on the way to becoming a philosophy of desire.

These reflections do not sound very Freudian and, indeed, they are not. They develop the implications that inhere in the concept of narcissism from its very first usage. What I am arguing is that Freud himself develops these implications and embodies them in the theory of the Eros and death instincts, thus making them part of the orthodox canon of psychoanalytic theory. Freud's later treatment of narcissism itself shows his movement in the direction I have suggested. Witness this passage from *Group Psychology and the Analysis of the Ego*, written shortly after *Beyond the Pleasure Principle*.

> By being born, we have made the step from an absolutely self-sufficient narcissism to the perception of a changing external world and the beginning of the discovery of objects. And with this is connected the fact that we cannot endure this new state of things for long, but that we periodically revert from it, in our sleep, to our former condition of absence of stimulation and avoidance of objects.[22]

This is the point from which Otto Rank took flight to travel in directions Freud did not find altogether to his liking. But the alternatives of "being" and "nothingness" that developed from a reflection on the nature of desire are exactly what Freud himself articulates in a more rudimentary and comprehensive fashion in *Beyond the Pleasure Principle*. For what lies beyond the pleasure principle is the "Nirvana principle" that governs the death instincts—namely, the striving that culminates in a cessation of striving. Indeed, the language Freud uses to characterize the Eros and death instincts is distinctly reminiscent of his discussion of the two phases of paranoia—the phase of narcissistic withdrawal from the world, which "happens silently," and the phase of recovery of relations with the world, which "forces itself so noisily upon our attention." Similarly, we learn in the discussion of instinct theory found in *The Ego and the Id* that the "death instincts are by their nature mute . . . the clamor of life proceeds for the most part from Eros."[23]

Whether or not it is from Eros that the clamor of life proceeds, it is clear, I think, that it is from a reflection on the essence of desire, captured by Freud in the concept of narcissism, that the theory of the Eros and death instincts proceeds. In this theory a philosophy of desire itself becomes the ground for the interpretation of organic existence in general—an existence to which, by virtue of Darwin's achievement, human reality is delivered. The vacillations of desire between appearing as meaning and being nothing is what Freud develops into the principles of two classes of instinct in opposition. Under the death instincts, Freud articulates desire's tendency toward self-nihilation—desire's disappearance in its act of realization. In polar opposition stands Eros—the "preserver of all things"—in which desire's longing to be, awakened from its self-possession by external disturbing forces, creates a forward thrust toward the objects of desire in which it finds its own image.

Tellingly, in this respect, Freud ends *Beyond the Pleasure Principle* with a speculation on the origins of sexuality, whose aim he earlier dissociates from the death instincts' aim of restoring an earlier state of things. This speculation explains the origins of sexuality on that very basis. Freud turns to the myth "which Plato puts into the mouth of Aristophanes in the *Symposium,* and which deals not only with the *origin* of the sexual instinct but also with the most important of its variations in relation to its object."

'The original human nature was not like the present, but different. In the first place, the sexes were originally three in number, not two as they are now; there was man, woman, and the union of the two. . . .' Everything about these primaeval men was double: they had four hands and four feet, two faces, two privy parts, and so on. Eventually Zeus decided to cut these men in two, 'like a sorb-apple which is halved for pickling.' After the division has been made, 'the two parts of man, each desiring his other half, came together, and threw their arms about one another eager to grow into one.'

Freud uses this myth to propose the hypothesis that "living substance at the time of its coming to life was torn apart into small particles, which have ever since endeavoured to reunite through the sexual instincts."[24] Here the Nothing that stands beyond life in death and the Everything that stands beyond life's longing for itself in the consummation of desire show themselves to be identical.

CHAPTER 11

Freud's Return:
The Psychoanalytic Odyssey

The key fact in the final development of Freud's thought is the transfiguration of its author's identity as a thinker. The nature of this transfiguration is delineated in reflections at the end of his life on the course of his development. In the 1935 postscript to *An Autobiographical Study* (1925), Freud finds that in his later years "a significant change has come about. Threads which in the course of my development had become intertangled have now begun to separate; interests which I had acquired in the later part of my life have receded, while the older and original ones become prominent once more." Thus, Freud tells us, "since I put forward my hypothesis of the existence of two classes of instincts (Eros and death instinct) and since I proposed a division of the mental personality into an ego, super-ego and id, I have made no further decisive contributions to psycho-analysis."

The two contributions Freud refers to were made in *Beyond the Pleasure Principle* and *The Ego and the Id* respectively. Looking backward, Freud sees these two phases in the unfolding of his final conception of mental life as exceptions to the dominant concerns of his later works. "This circumstance is connected," he continues, "with *an alteration in myself*, with what might be described as *a phase of regressive development*" (my italics). To express the relation of this "phase of regressive development" to what preceded it, Freud invokes a familiar image. "My interest," he tells us, "after making a lifelong *détour* through the natural sciences, medicine and psychotherapy, returned to the cultural problems which had fascinated me long before, when I was a youth scarcely old enough for thinking."

The image of a detour echoes the one Freud used almost forty years earlier when he confessed to Fleiss that by following a "circuitous route" from medicine to psychology, he secretly nursed the hope of realizing his youthful passion and original objective, philosophy. Freud now identifies *Totem and Taboo* as the point where he ended his "lifelong *détour*" and set foot on the path to solving the problems that had fascinated him as a youth. "At the very climax of my psycho-analytic work, in 1912, I already attempted in *Totem and Taboo* to make use of the newly discovered findings of analysis in order to investigate the origins of religion and morality. I now carried this work a stage further in two later essays, *The Future of an Illusion* (1927) and *Civilization and Its Discontents* (1930)." The beginnings of Freud's final phase of development thus coincide with the climactic moments of his strictly psychoanalytic work. "I perceived ever more clearly," he continues, "that the events of human history, the interaction between human nature, cultural development and the precipitates of primaeval experiences (the most prominent of which is religion), are no more than a reflection of the dynamic conflicts between the ego, the id and the super-ego, which psycho-analysis studies in the individual—are the very same processes repeated upon a wider stage." Thus, the phase of development that marks the reemergence of Freud's original interests is focused upon the events of human history—events that are repetitions "upon a wider stage" of internal conflicts of the mind. "In *The Future of an Illusion*," he concludes, "I expressed an essentially negative valuation of religion. Later, I found a formula which did better justice to it: while granting that its power lies in the truth which it contains, I showed that that truth was not a material but a historical truth."[1]

These reflections constitute a remarkable revelation of the final disposition of Freud's thought. They cast, I think, a definitive light on the venture launched in *The Interpretation of Dreams*. Looking back from the end of his journey, Freud sees the psychology of the unconscious as but another leg of a circuitous route to the resolution of his earliest concerns. The strictly psychoanalytic phase of development now appears as a prolegomena to what followed—as a long period of preparation for the achievement of his oldest, original objectives in "studies which, though they originate in psycho-analysis, stretch far beyond it."[2]

That in the course of the psychoanalytic venture Freud would at some point come to address cultural problems is not, of course, an unexpected turn of events. From the outset, in 1901, Freud had sighted the cultural realm and fixed it in a definite relation to psychoanalysis. The relevant passage in *The Psychopathology of Everyday Life*, let us recall, asserts that

> "a large part of the mythological view of the world, which extends a long way into the most modern religions, *is nothing but psychology projected into the external world*. The obscure recognition ... of psychical factors and relations in the unconscious is mirrored—it is difficult to express it in other terms and here the analogy with paranoia must come to our aid—in the construction of a *supernatural reality*, which is destined to be changed back once more by science into the *psychology of the unconscious.*

Thus Freud sights the prospect of transforming "*metaphysics* into *metapsychology.*"[3]

These formulations, we noted earlier, already indicate Freud's deferment of the problems of culture to a later point. If the construction of a supernatural reality is to be changed back once more *by science* into the psychology of the unconscious, Freud had first to be in possession of the psychology of the unconscious *as* a science. Only then could he turn to the domain of mythico-religious meanings and, applying the psychology of the unconscious to them, hope to appropriate them within the cognitions of science. But the 1901 passage also tells us something else, whose significance stands forth clearly in the light of Freud's retrospective reflections of 1935. The transformation of metaphysics into metapsychology stands not merely as a harbinger of things to come but as a landmark of something that had already by 1901 been realized—namely, the fate religion had suffered at the hands of science. For what else does Freud mean when he tells us that the construction of a supernatural reality is *destined* to be changed back into the psychology of the unconscious? Where was it that Freud had read this destiny? Since, as *An Autobiographical Study* also tells us, Freud's submission to the authority of science was preceded by a "deep engrossment with the Bible story,"[4] what else are we to infer but that Freud had read that destiny within himself and then recognized in this personal destiny the fate of his times? Returning from his long detour to explain scientifically the origin of religion in *Totem and Taboo*, Freud sought to transform this personal destiny into a shared truth. In this light, psychoanalysis is no mere reflection of its times. In pursuing the psychoanalytic venture, Freud sought to turn himself into the instrument of the *Zeitgeist*. As the path to understanding religion from a scientific standpoint, psychoanalysis constitutes a vehicle for secularization. As a scientific substitute for the religious vision of man's fate, psychoanalysis becomes the philosophy of a world whose gods have fled.

The upshot of these considerations is that it is simply wrong to treat *Totem and Taboo* as the application of psychoanalysis to a cognate field outside its main area of competence and interest. On the contrary, the problems Freud finally addressed in *Totem and Taboo* are the ones that provoked the psychoanalytic venture in the first place. That venture finds its authentic realization in Freud's cultural phase of development. The reality principle, whose extrapolation first secures Freud's return to the domain of culture, merely conceptualizes at the level of biological discourse the primordial but still "unconscious" intuition that gave birth to the psychoanalytic perspective: the victory of science over religion. That is why psychoanalysis begins with a disavowal of metaphysics and why the reality principle marks Freud's return to this point of departure. The reality principle is the scientific sublimation of a crucial experience in Freud's contemplative life—the experience of disillusionment with metaphysics, of loss of faith in a transcendent reality.

We are thus in a position to define the genesis of the psychoanalytic venture in the following manner. Since as a youth Freud had been deeply moved by religious meanings, his later submission to the authority of science necessarily cast a dark shadow across those meanings and rendered them opaque to the understanding. That is, in the face of science's self-certainty of the creaturely origins and destiny of man, the whole realm of prescientific understandings of the world, and of man's relation to it, lost its reality force—which is to say, its authority. The scientific self-certainty still lives in our times and is what leads G. G. Simpson, the leading evolutionist of our day, to make the unequivocal assertion that "all attempts to answer [the question 'What is man?'] before 1859 [viz., before the publication of Darwin's *Origin*] are worthless and . . . we will be better off if we ignore them completely."[5] For Freud, however, science's self-certainty of the natural provenance of man does not mean that we should ignore the prescientific self-interpretations of man. "What the whole of mankind has believed for centuries surely cannot be nonsense;" he had written his fiancee in 1882, "it must have some meaning."[6] Deprived of their lifeblood by science, such meanings become the fossil remains of man's phylogenetic travail that litter the landscape of his prescientific past. As products of the human mind, however, they command both our respect and our attention. For they attest to the fact that, as a *biological* being, mankind has lived a reality that lies beyond the realm of biological necessity—the reality of a shared world of meaning. They thus pertain to man's being as a species of animal that is mindful of its being.

A question arises here, however. If the problem of making sense of religious phenomena from the standpoint of science prompted Freud's venture in the first place, why did he seek his answers by way of a long detour through the depths of the unconscious? If the psychology of religious belief was his deepest concern, why did he not address himself to religious phenomena from the outset? The answer has to do with the way in which religion presented itself as a problem calling for the work of interpretation in the first place. The most elementary consequence of the self-certainty of science is that "external reality" is entirely *devoid* of meaning. "The moment one enquires about the sense or value of life he is sick," Freud wrote in his later years, "since objectively neither of them has any existence."[7] And the reason that the question of the sense or value of life has no objective standing is that natural science's disclosure of a nature with man in it bore the unmistakable implication that man's appearance within nature was fortuitous. For as a science of efficient causes, the science of Enlightenment forbids the questioner who has submitted to its discipline to ask the question, "For what purpose?" or "To what end?" Science simply rules such questions out of court. And that is why the objective reality of nature disclosed by natural science is a reality wholly indifferent to human purposes, concerns, or interests.

The shadow that science cast upon Freud's youthful religious involvements thus transposed the problem of interpreting prescientific meanings into the problem of interpreting a self that could be moved by such meanings. For the necessary correlate to science's disclosure that nature is itself devoid of meaning is that all meaning is psychogenic—that it must arise from the depths of human subjectivity. The psychology of the unconscious, the science of a self that finds itself moved by meanings that have proved to be illusory, was thus a necessary condition for the scientific interpretation of man's prescientific perceptions of a world imbued with meaning. In the very way science raised the problem of meaning, Freud could begin his pursuit of meaning only with a *Quaestio mihi factus sum*, with the question I have become for myself.

This is exactly the understanding Freud expresses in those same passages in *The Psychopathology of Everyday Life* where he first arrives at the idea of transforming metaphysics into metapsychology. He prepares the reader for that formulation with the example of the everyday paranoiac—the superstitious person. The contrast Freud draws between his own scientific outlook and the mundane metaphysics of superstition is revealing. The superstitious person, we learn,

> has a tendency to ascribe to *external chance happenings a meaning* which will become manifest in real events, and to regard such chance happenings as a means of expressing something that is hidden from him in the external world. The differences between myself and the superstitious person are two: First, he *projects outwards* a motivation which *I look for within*. Secondly, he interprets *chance* as due to an *event* while I trace it back to a *thought*. But what is *hidden* from him [viz., the meaning behind the fortuitous event] corresponds to what is *unconscious* for me, and the *compulsion* not to let chance count as chance but to interpret it is common to both of us. [my italics][8]

Thus, the eclipse of metaphysical meaning by science that called Freud to the work of interpretation required him to begin by looking within to interpret a self that could be moved by such meaning—that self being quite literally Freud's own, a self whose fascination with religious meaning had been succeeded by a submission to the authority of science.

In depriving him of his religious illusions, then, science posed for Freud a *Quaestio mihi factus sum*. The self that science thus threw into question, however, was not a self sustained by a world. On the contrary, the very problem science posed for the self was that its relations with the world were void. Having exposed the emptiness of his religious involvements, science deprived Freud of a world per se. His was the situation described by Nietzsche in *Twilight of the Idols*. "The true world—we have abolished. What world has remained? The apparent one perhaps? But no! *With the true world we have also abolished the apparent one!*"[9] Science's eclipse of the "true world" of transcendent meaning had cast a shadow on *this* world, the "apparent one." That is to say, with the loss of a transcendent ground, the hierarchy of values that makes sense of the vagaries of everyday experience and organizes them into a world collapses, and the world of appearance in which our daily lives transpire dissolves into an inchoate flux. To pursue the quest for meaning, Freud had first to displace the locus of meaning from external reality to a worldless within. The psychology of the unconscious is founded by the occlusion of the ego and its wordly involvements because the standpoint of science, by its very nature, deprives meaning of its wordly status.

How did Freud accomplish this displacement, which is itself prior to the work of interpretation? He accomplished it by following the lead of that natural science which is concerned with our perception of the world, the science of optics. Newton's *Opticks*, which is paradigmatic of natural science's outlook in this field, can help us understand the path Freud took. Newton's natural-scientific account of perception is as follows:

> When a man views any object, that light which comes from the several points of the object is so defracted by the transparent skins and humors of the eye . . . as to converge and meet again at so many points in the bottom of the eye, and there to paint the picture of the object upon that skin . . . with which the bottom of the eye is covered. . . . And these pictures propagated along the fibers of the optic nerves into the brain are the cause of vision.[10]

According to this theory, it is not the objects themselves that are seen in the act of vision. Rather, "the images only carried through the organs of sense into our little sensoriums, *are there seen and beheld by that which in us perceives and thinks*" (my italics).[11] What we should note here is the homunculus problem Newton falls into—which is virtually unavoidable for a science that must explain vision in terms of causal connections within material nature. Phenomenologically speaking, things simply appear. I see them. But for a science of external reality that identifies perception with the translation of motion along the material organs of sense, things are not so simple. Behind the appearance of things lies the material reality of the points of light reflected off the object which strike the eye and transmit the "image" of the object through the organs of sense, at whose terminus it is not "I" who sees this image but "that which" is in me that perceives and thinks. If this perceiver within me is itself an "I," then it is not the phenomenal "I" of experience but a transcendental "I" that stands beyond the phenomenal reality of the world. If not, then I myself must perceive this something within me that perceives the image of the object. Hence the famous homunculus problem whereby I am forced to conceive of a little man standing inside my head who does my perceiving for me. The inevitable consequence of this natural-scientific explanation of perception is to transpose the experience of perception—and with it the appearance of things—from the world to some point within me, just as Freud transposes the appearance and experience of meaning from the external world to the internal locus of the "true psychical reality," the unconscious.

This analogy between the science of optics and the science of the unconscious is not merely a conjecture. Freud's first attempt to get a fix on the unconscious in chapter 7 of the dream book uses the "analogy of a compound microscope or a photographic apparatus" to present the "idea of psychical locality" needed to picture the "mental apparatus" capable of producing dreams. Freud bases this analogy on the insight of Gustav Fechner that "*the scene of action of dreams is different from that of waking ideational life.*" The analogy with optical mechanics serves here to identify the oneiric "scene of action" as a psychical locality that corresponds "to a point inside the apparatus."[12] Just as optical mechanics transposes the locus of the visual experience to a point inside the brain, to which the image of the object is transmitted by the perceptual apparatus, so Freud transposes the locus of meaning to a point inside the mind— to the oneiric scene of action, the unconscious. All that is different in Freud's analogy is that the camera takes the place of Newton's eye.

A further question arises at this point, and it is the decisive one for understanding Freud's odyssey. Having explored the worldless depths of the unconscious with scientifically chastened eyes, Freud returns in *Totem and Taboo* to address the problem of the origins of religion and morality. The result, however, is not the appropriation of metaphysical meanings within the science of the unconscious. On the contrary, in order to "apply" the psychology of the unconscious to those meanings, Freud is first required to introduce a fundamental new concept into his theory—that of narcissism. And in the wake of introducing narcissism, Freud's theory of mental life undergoes a radical reconceptualization. We can sharpen what is at stake in this metamorphosis. When Freud finally comes to complete the reconceptualization of psychoanalytic theory in *The Ego and the Id*, he begins by abolishing the unconscious as a systematic concept and substantive reality. Concluding his discussion of the various senses of the unconscious, he writes, "we must admit that the characteristic of being unconscious begins to lose significance for us. It becomes a quality which we are unable to make, as we should have hoped to do, the basis of far-reaching and inevitable conclusions."[13] What takes the place of what Freud had originally identified as the locus of the true psychical reality is not so much the id as the conflicts of the Eros and death instincts, which, henceforward, Freud draws upon as the basis of psychical manifestations and, in particular, the projections of culture. The "meaning of the evolution of civilization [Kultur]," he announces in *Civilization and Its Discontents*, "is no longer obscure to us. It must present the struggle between Eros and Death, between the instinct of life and the instinct of destruction, as it works itself out in the human species."[14]

The final development of Freud's thought thus presents us with the following ironic situation: in order to transform metaphysics into metapsychology, Freud is finally required to transform his science of the unconscious into the mythology of the Eros and death instincts. In 1932 Freud admits to having carried out this transformation. "But does not every science come in the end to a kind of mythology like this?" he asks Einstein rhetorically. Our question is not a rhetorical but a substantive one. What in the origins of the psychoanalytic venture accounts for this outcome? The fact that the displacement of meaning that had opened up the domain of the unconscious had also created a blind spot in Freud's theoretical vision. The transformation of Freud's science into a mythology was the consequence of Freud's confrontation with and overcoming of this blind spot by the introduction of the concept of narcissism. How so?

The self-certainty of science that the world is devoid of meaning is what requires the displacement of meaning from the world to the depths of the unconscious. In order to bring his own theoretical vision into conformity with the standpoint of science, Freud had to situate himself at a point external to the concerns and interests of the human life-world. Only from an objective standpoint independent of the everyday manifestations of mind could he proceed to conduct his investigation of mental life with scientific certainty. The unconscious is first and foremost a *theoretical* construct designed to meet the demands of scientific impartiality. It is the epistemic space which affords a look at mental phenomena in their objectivity as impulses arising from the body. The disclosure of repressed meaning, attained in the blotting out of the "I" of everyday existence, provides the data which Freud then fixes within the objective framework that secures and grounds them—namely, the theory of psychosexual development underwritten by the biological hypothesis.

With the displacement of meaning that accompanies the founding of the psychoanalytic perspective, the appearance of worldly meaning is necessarily construed as a projective illusion of psychical factors and relations that have their true reality in the worldless depths of the unconscious. Hence, echoing his 1901 formulations, Freud informs us in the second essay of *Totem and Taboo* that,

> under conditions whose nature has not yet been sufficiently established, internal perceptions of emotional and thought processes can be projected outwards; they are thus employed for building up the external world, though they should by rights remain part of the *internal* world. . . . [O]wing to the projection outwards of internal perceptions, primitive men arrived at a picture of the external world which we, with our intensified conscious perception, have to translate back into psychology.[15]

The meaning lived by the primitive man is nothing but a "reflection of the mental world [which] is bound to blot out the other picture of the world—the one which *we* seem to perceive."[16] The world which *we*, that is to say, men of scientifically disciplined vision, *seem* to see (and here Freud's ambivalence already betrays a recognition of the problem with this understanding) is nothing but the world in its naked positivity—a world indifferent to human wishes and to the meaning they sustain.

It is exactly here that the displacement of meaning at the outset of the psychoanalytic venture creates a blind spot in Freud's theoretical vision. For, if meaning is but a projection upon the flux of a "changing external world"[17]—a world that "in reality" is devoid of meaning—then the meaning of science cannot appear within science's own field of vision. And, indeed, in *Totem and Taboo* it does not. *Totem and Taboo* is not science's reflection on itself but a reflection on the meanings science has surpassed from the standpoint of science's vision of a world devoid of meaning. But in order to gain a purchase on the prescientific understandings of the world, Freud had to elevate his vision beyond the positivistic realm of biological necessity. Introducing the concept of narcissism to account for the appearance of meaning from without, Freud fixed his gaze on the domain of worldly meaning from which he had been exiled by science. Once he had done this, it was all but inevitable that he would come to see that the meaning of being biological—a *fact* presented to man by Darwin as the *essential* fact of his being—could be realized only in the locus of meaning that subsists between self and world. The world asserted its primordial reality, which even the objectivity of science cannot surpass. For by the very ground of certainty science afforded him, Freud knew that the meaning of science, which had prompted his theoretical odyssey, was itself no illusory projection. That meaning had appeared with all the necessity of fate when, through Darwin, science presented to man the stark facts of life.

Thus, midway in his course, Freud was brought face to face with the deepest motives and intuitions of his theoretical odyssey. "I am growing more and more convinced of the cultural value [actually Freud makes a slip of the pen here and uses the word *Welt* instead of *Wert*] of psycho-analysis," he wrote Jung in July of 1910, "and I long for the lucid mind that will draw from it the justified inferences for philosophy and sociology. I am under the impression—but perhaps this is only a projection of my present listless state of mind—that we have come to a standstill for the moment and are waiting for some new impetus. But I am not impatient."[18]

What Freud confronted in this impasse was a task he had not anticipated—the task of reconstructing from a scientific standpoint the world that science had abolished. A few months later he prepares himself for that task by engaging in the analysis of paranoia that opened the way to *Totem and Taboo*. And to characterize this pathology of projected meaning, he turns to some passages from Goethe's *Faust*.

After Faust has uttered the curses which free him from the world, the Chorus of Spirits sings:

Woe! Woe!
Thou hast it destroyed,
The beautiful world
With powerful fist!
In ruins 'tis hurled,
By the blow of a demi-god shattered!

Mightier
For the children of men
More splendid
Build it again
In thine own bosom build it anew!

And the paranoiac builds it again, not more splendid, it is true but at
least so he can once more live in it. He builds it up by the work of his
delusions.[19]

So, too, Freud begins to build the world anew, not, to be sure, as a
paranoiac delusion or a newfangled religion, but as a scientific understanding of the human situation for men whose world has been
deprived of its metaphysical sanctions by science. If *The Interpretation of Dreams* and the *Three Essays* exposed desire to be the
animal essence of human existence, *Totem and Taboo* added that
a conflict at the heart of desire makes man the kind of animal he is.
In delineating the instinctual sources of the feeling of guilt and the
need for authority, the psychoanalytic revolution culminates in a
profoundly conservative reaffirmation of a tradition that had lost its
authority.

What we witness in the final development of Freud's thought is
the transfiguration of Freud's theoretical persona, the metamorphosis of a natural scientist into a philosopher. With this, Freud's odyssey reaches its destination. Freud returns to his original goal and
place of origin, philosophy.

How are we to square this return to philosophy with what we
learned about the insight that provoked Freud's odyssey, about his
recognition of Darwin's closure of the metaphysical horizon, about
Freud's disavowal of metaphysics? The answer is, Freud finally
owns up to that disavowal. In his final development neither his
commitment to natural science nor his disavowal of metaphysics is
abandoned. On the contrary, they are pursued to ever more radical
consequences. The intent of his cultural essays, *Totem and Taboo*,
The Future of an Illusion, and *Civilization and Its Discontents*,
is to seal the fate of metaphysics once and for all. Correspondingly,

the ego psychology that emerges in this period is the psychology of European man living in the aftermath of the Christian era, a guide to the mental labyrinth that the death of God left in its wake. In the end as in the beginning, psychoanalysis articulates a discipline of being governed by the authority of science. What Freud's final development brings to fulfillment is the philosophical animus that led him to turn from metaphysics to science in the first place. Freud becomes a philosopher because the intended effect of his final theories is to substitute science for metaphysics, to insert science into the void that the demise of metaphysics had opened in the cultural world of Western humanity.

Notes

SE-*The Standard Edition of the Complete Psychological Works of Sigmund Freud*, ed. James Strachey, 24 vols. (London: Hogarth Press, 1953–74).

Chapter 1

1. SE XIV, "Instincts and Their Vicissitudes," p. 134.
2. *The Letters of Sigmund Freud, 1873–1939*, ed. Ernst L. Freud (London: Hogarth Press, 1970), letter 176, June 6, 1917, p. 324.
3. Hannah Arendt, "Tradition and the Modern Age," in *Between Past and Future* (New York: Viking Press, 1961), p. 25.
4. SE XV, *Introductory Lectures on Psychoanalysis*, pp. 16–17.
5. Ibid., p. 17.
6. SE XXII, *New Introductory Lectures on Psychoanalysis*, p. 68.
7. SE XV, p. 18.
8. Ibid., p. 40.
9. Ibid., p. 87.
10. Ibid., p. 21; see also SE VII, *Three Essays on the Theory of Sexuality*, p. 131, and SE XIII, "The Claims of Psychoanalysis to Scientific Interest," pp. 181–82.
11. SE XIX, *The Ego and the Id*, p. 19.
12. SE XIII, "The Claims of Psychoanalysis to Scientific Interest," p. 179.
13. SE XXIII, *An Outline of Psychoanalysis*, pp. 144 and 157.
14. SE XXI, *The Future of an Illusion*, pp. 55–56.
15. Raymond E. Fancher, *Psychoanalytic Psychology* (New York: W. W. Norton, 1973), p. 96.
16. SE XX, *An Autobiographical Study*, pp. 58–59.
17. SE XXIII, *An Outline of Psychoanalysis*, p. 196.
18. Jürgen Habermas, *Knowledge and Human Interests*, trans. Jeremy Shapiro (Boston: Beacon Press, 1971), p. 252.

154

Notes to Pages 13–20

19. Ibid., p. 259.
20. Ibid., p. 253.
21. Ibid., p. 254.
22. Ibid., p. 228.
23. We should note here, however, that Habermas does not simply discard the idea of a metapsychology. Having exposed the "scientism" that informs Freud's metapsychology, Habermas seeks to put in its place a new metapsychology—a metapsychology that makes explicit the "intention of enlightenment" which informs the analytic dialogue. "Here we are dealing not with an empirical theory, but a metatheory, or, better, *metahermeneutics*, which explicates the conditions of possibility of psychoanalytic knowledge. Metapsychology unfolds *the logic of interpretation in the analytic situation of dialogue*" (p. 254, Habermas).
24. Paul Ricoeur, *Freud and Philosophy*, trans. Denis Savage (New Haven: Yale University Press, 1970), p. 65.
25. Ibid., p. 66.
26. SE I, "Extracts from the Fleiss Papers," p. 274.
27. SE VII, *Three Essays*, p. 168, n. 2.
28. Habermas, *Knowledge and Human Interests*, p. 256.

Chapter 2

1. John Dewey, "The Influence of Darwin on Philosophy," in *The Influence of Darwin on Philosophy and Other Essays in Contemporary Thought* (Bloomington: Indiana University Press, 1910), p. 19.
2. SE XX, *An Autobiographical Study*, p. 8.
3. SE XVII, "A Difficulty in the Path of Psychoanalysis," pp. 140–41.
4. Charles Darwin, *The Origin of Species by Means of Natural Selection* (1859; reprint ed., Middlesex: Penguin, 1968), p. 458.
5. Ibid., p. 236.
6. John Herman Randall, "The Changing Impact of Darwinism on Philosophy," *Journal of the History of Ideas* 22 (1961): 454.
7. While the heart of biological theory has remained Darwinian, the program for an evolutionary psychology has never been carried to a successful conclusion. E. O. Wilson's *Sociobiology* has been the focus of the contemporary debate.
8. It is on this point that Frank Sulloway's *Freud, Biologist of the Mind* (New York: Basic Books, 1979) goes wrong. The problem is indicated in the title, since Freud is not a biologist of the mind. He is a psychologist of the body.
9. An important exception is Freud's discovery that his patient's childhood sexual experiences turned out to be fantasies. Letter 69, Sept. 21, 1897, to Wilhelm Fleiss in *The Origins of Psychoanalysis; Letters to Wilhelm Fleiss, Drafts and Notes: 1887–1902*, ed. Marie Bonaparte, Anna Freud, and Ernst Kris (New York: Basic Books, 1954), pp. 215–18.
10. SE I, "Project for a Scientific Psychology," p. 295. A translation of

the "Project" is also found in the volume of letters to Fleiss mentioned in the previous note, but the translation in the *Standard Edition* is based on a closer editorial scrutiny of Freud's original handwriting.

11. SE I, "Project," p. 307.

12. Ibid., p. 295.

13. Habermas, *Knowledge and Human Interests*, p. 252.

14. SE I, "Project," pp. 315–16.

15. Ibid., p. 317.

16. SE VII, *Three Essays* (3d ed.), p. 168.

17. Quoted in John C. Burnham, "Instinct Theory and the German Reaction to Weismannism," *Journal of the History of Biology* 5:2 (Fall 1972): 324.

18. SE VII, *Three Essays* (3d ed.), p. 131.

19. Sandor Ferenczi, "The Scientific Importance of Freud's *Three Essays on the Theory of Sexuality*," trans. from the German by Christian Lenhardt from *Internationale Zeitschrift für Ärtzliche Psychoanalyse* 3 (1915): 228.

20. René Descartes, *Discourse on Method*, in *The Philosophical Works of Descartes*, trans. Elizabeth S. Haldane and G. R. T. Ross (Cambridge: Cambridge University Press, 1972), vol. 1, p. 101.

21. E. A. Burtt, *The Metaphysical Foundations of Modern Science*, rev. ed. (Garden City: Doubleday, 1954), p. 105.

22. Hans Jonas, *The Phenomenon of Life* (New York: Delta, 1966), p. 53.

23. Ibid., p. 53.

24. Ibid., p. 53.

25. Ibid., pp. 53–54.

26. Ibid., p. 55.

27. Ibid., p. 55; cf. Burtt, *The Metaphysical Foundations*, chaps. 3 and 4, for a fuller treatment.

28. Ibid., p. 55.

29. Ibid., p. 56.

30. Ibid., p. 57.

31. Ibid., p. 58.

32. Cf. Descartes, *Meditations on First Philosophy*, p. 149.

33. Ernst Haeckel, *The Riddle of the Universe at the Close of the Nineteenth Century*, trans. J. McCabe (New York: Harper, 1900), p. 245.

34. SE I, "Extracts," letter 84, p. 274.

35. Except for an early published use of the term (1901), which we take up in its place, metapsychology does not appear again in Freud's writings until 1915. The current passage contains the first use of the term in which its meaning can be discerned.

36. Freud, *The Origins of Psychoanalysis*, letter 121, Oct. 11, 1899, p. 300.

37. Ernest Jones, *Sigmund Freud: Life and Works*, 3 vols. (London: Hogarth Press, 1962), vol. 2, p. 319.

Chapter 3

1. SE II, *Studies on Hysteria*, with Joseph Breuer, p. xxxi.
2. An illuminating discussion of the "reciprocal effect of theory and practice" is found in chap. 4 of *The Development of Psychoanalysis* (New York: Dover, 1923), by Sandor Ferenczi and Otto Rank. These two close disciples of Freud note that "one of the peculiarities of psychoanalysis" is that "the scientific instrument is at the same time the curative one," and they characterize the relation of knowledge and technique as "a benign circle of mutual beneficial influence of the practice upon the theory and the theory upon the practice."
3. SE II, *Studies*, p. 123.
4. Ibid., p. 6.
5. Ibid., p. 124.
6. Ibid., p. 6.
7. Ibid., p. 7.
8. SE III, "Further Remarks on the Psychoneuroses," p. 171.
9. Cf. SE II, *Studies*, p. 45n.
10. SE V, *The Interpretation of Dreams*, p. 615.
11. Ibid., p. 613.
12. SE II, *Studies*, p. 287.
13. Ibid., p. 300.
14. Ibid., p. 301.
15. Ibid., p. 293.
16. Ibid., pp. 292–93.
17. SE IV, *The Interpretation of Dreams*, pp. 100–01.
18. SE XV, *Introductory Lectures*, p. 83.
19. Ibid., pp. 21–22.
20. SE V, *Interpretation*, p. 613. After his death, a copy of Kant's *Critique of Pure Reason*, signed and dated 1882, was one of the few major works of philosophy found in Freud's library. Cf. "The Freud Library," by Harry Trosman and Roger Dennis Simmons, *American Psychoanalytic Association Journal* 21 (1973): 653–55.
21. SE V, *Interpretation*, p. 615. My contention is that the silent but ubiquitous presence of the body as the inward ground of mind governs all the peculiar twistings and bendings psychoanalytic theory imposes on the framework of dualism within which Freud tries to unfold his thought. In the present case, this is seen in the inversion of the relation of conscious and unconscious as that relation stands in the reflective logic of the analytic dialogue. Further evidence for the contention that Freud's positing of the body is the basis of this inversion is found in the "Project for a Scientific Psychology," where the assertion that consciousness is *not* the primary reality already occurs. Significantly, the "Project" was written in the same year that the *Studies* were published—that is, in the same period when the theory of the psychoneuroses was worked out.

As we recall, in the "Project" Freud tries to develop a psychology that will qualify as a natural science by *representing* psychical processes as quantitatively determinate states of specifiable material particles. It is indeed in the "Project" that Freud, without yet realizing its implications, makes the inwardness of the body a matter for reflective investigation by positing the body as the source of the stimuli that, arising from the interior of the system, sustain all psychical activity. But we also find in the "Project" the statement, which is striking in the context of our present concerns, that the "neuronal processes" by which the "Project" represents psychical activity are "in the first instance to be regraded to their whole extent as unconscious and are to be inferred like other material things" (SE I, p. 308).

The editor of the *Standard Edition* rightly notes that "this is a statement made about *physiological* entities—'neuronal processes.' Some time was still to elapse before Freud could make exactly the same statement about *psychical* events" (SE I, p. 308, n. 2, editor's italics). Without denying the validity of the editor's measured comments, we must nonetheless not allow it to lead us to the conclusion that the distinctively psychoanalytic orientation established by the dream book arises merely from the translation into psychological terms of conclusions earlier arrived at concerning physiological processes. The translation indeed occurs in *The Interpretation of Dreams*, but its significance becomes clear only when we see it *in combination with* the inversion the dream book executes in the relationship between unconscious and conscious.

One aspect of the translation from a neuronal characterization of the unconscious to a psychical one is the acknowledgment of the espistemological priority of consciousness. Let us remember that it was from consciousness that neuronal processes discussed in the "Project" were inferred in the first place. Thus, as we read in a typical formulation of the psychoanalytic period proper:

> As far as [the] physical characteristics [of unconscious processes] are concerned, they are totally inaccessible to us: no physiological concept or chemical process can give us any notion of their nature. On the other hand, we know for certain that they have abundant points of contact with conscious mental processes, and all the categories which we employ to describe conscious mental acts, such as ideas, purposes, resolutions and so on, can be applied to them. [SE XIV, "The Unconscious," p. 168]

Since what Freud translates from physical into psychological categories in the movement from the "Project" to the dream book is not merely the unconscious but the assertion of its *primacy*, however, we can see that the body must still inhere in what is being translated. How so? The translation itself is made possible only by the opening of unconscious depths from the side of consciousness as exemplified in the *Studies*. The *inversion* of the relationship between surface and depth—the shift from the unconscious as a negative moment in the ego's self-explication to the unconscious as a positive manifestation of the true psychical reality hidden in the depths—is made possible only by the translation of the body into the psychical domain. Only the presence of the body can explain the shift of the psychical center of gravity from the surface to the depths of the mind.

22. SE XIII, "The Claims of Psychoanalysis to Scientific Interest," p. 181.

23. SE II, *Studies*, p. 161.
24. Ibid., p. 288.
25. Ibid., p. 288.
26. Ibid., p. 124.
27. Cf. SE XII, "Remembering, Repeating and Working Through," p. 150.
28. Habermas, *Knowledge and Human Interests*, p. 259.
29. Ibid., p. 260.
30. Wilhelm Dilthey, *Pattern and Meaning in History*, trans. and ed. H. P. Rickman (New York: Harper & Row, 1961), p. 107, a compilation of major passages from vol. 7 of Dilthey's *Gesammelte Schriften* (Stuttgart: Teubner, 1914–36).
32. Ibid., p. 127.
33. Ibid., p. 73.
34. Ibid., p. 98.
35. Ibid., p. 168.
36. Ibid., p. 73.
37. Ibid., p. 85.
38. Ibid., p. 87.
39. Ibid., p. 89.
40. Ibid., p. 126.
41. Ibid., p. 89.
42. Ibid., p. 89.
43. Cf. Habermas, *Knowledge and Human Interests*. Habermas gives concise expression to the difference between Freud and Dilthey.

> Dilthey had conceived life-historical meaning as the condition of possible hermeneutic understanding, thus tying understanding to conscious intentions. Freud comes upon systematic distortions of meaning which, for their part, do express intentions. But the latter must transcend what is subjectively thought. [Habermas, p. 217]

> Psychoanalytic interpretation is concerned with those connections of symbols in which a subject deceives itself about itself. The *depth hermeneutics* that Freud counterposes to Dilthey's philological hermeneutics deals with texts indicating *self-deceptions of the author*. [Habermas, p. 218]

However enlightening Habermas's designation of psychoanalysis as a "depth hermeneutics," it wholly obscures the fact that psychoanalytic theory points beyond the limits of reflection while trying to remain within a framework of understanding defined by reflection—viz., Cartesian dualism.
44. SE XVII, "A Difficulty in the Path of Psychoanalysis," pp. 141–43.
45. SE XIII, "Scientific Interest," p. 183.
46. SE XI, *Leonardo da Vinci*, p. 136.
47. SE XVII, "Lines of Advance in Psychoanalytic Therapy," p. 161.
48. Habermas, *Knowledge and Human Interests*, p. 233.
49. SE XVI, *Introductory Lectures*, p. 417.

50. François Jacob, *The Logic of Life*, trans. B. E. Spillmann (New York: Vintage, 1976), p. 296.
51. SE XIII, "Scientific Interest," p. 182.

Chapter 4

1. SE XII, p. 74. For a fuller discussion of this difficult point in Freud's theory cf. Hans W. Loewald, "On Motivation and Instinct Theory," in his *Papers on Psychoanalysis* (New Haven: Yale University Press, 1980), esp. pp. 114–24.
2. The incidental reference is in SE VII, *Three Essays*, p. 168; the quote is from SE XII, p. 74.
3. SE XIV, "On Narcissism: An Introduction," p. 78.
4. SE VII, *Three Essays*, p. 131.
5. SE XIV, "On Narcissism," pp. 78–79.
6. SE XXII, *Civilization and Its Discontents*, p. 117.
7. SE XIII, "Scientific Interest," p. 182.
8. SE XXIII, "Outline," p. 144.
9. *Letters of Sigmund Freud*, letter 176, p. 324.
10. SE XIV, "Instincts and Their Vicissitudes," pp. 118 and 122.
11. Dilthey is quoted in Herbert A. Hodges, *The Philosophy of Wilhelm Dilthey* (London: Routledge & Kegan Paul, 1952), p. 266.
12. SE VII, *Three Essays*, p. 135.
13. A certain irony in Freud's utilization of Weismann's theory is worth noting here. After *Totem and Taboo* Freud became an adherent of the Lamarckian hypothesis of the "inheritance of acquired characteristics." Thus, still in 1938, he writes in *Moses and Monotheism* of "the present attitude of biological science, which refuses to hear of the inheritance of acquired characteristics by succeeding generations." He continues, "I must, however, in all modesty confess that nevertheless I cannot do without this factor in biological evolution" (SE XXIII, p. 200). The irony here is that Weismann's theory of the germ-plasm (1892) was the basis for the definitive elimination of that explanatory factor from evolutionary theory—a fact Freud could not have failed to know. The very independence of the germ-plasm from the vicissitudes of the soma is what made this theory instrumental in that regard. Weismannism allows for no mechanism whereby wisdom in survival gained in the course of life can be passed on genetically from parent to offspring. Genetically determined variations in the offspring are the product of fortuitous mutations in the germ cells. Variation is random rather than shaped by the experience of forebears. Weismann thus provided the requisite genetic theory for the nonteleological mechanics of variation and natural selection. Cf. Robert A. Paul, "Did the Primal Crime Take Place?" (*Ethos* 4 [1976]: 311–52) for an evaluation of the Freudian position in light of recent biological advances. Generally, it should be noted, however, that the findings of molecular biology are taken to confirm the elimination of Lamarckism from evolutionary explanation. Cf. Ernst

Mayr, "Lamarck Revisited" (*Journal of the History of Biology* 5: 1 [Spring 1972]: 55–94).

14. SE XIV, "On Narcissism," p. 78.
15. SE XVI, *Introductory Lectures*, p. 413.
16. Darwin, *Origin of Species*, p. 136.
17. Cf. John F. Miller III, "The Logic of Evolution," *Southwestern Journal of Philosophy* 3: 1 (Spring 1972): 147–56 for an interesting discussion along these lines.
18. Darwin, pp. 130–31.
19. Ibid., p. 136.
20. Ludwig Binswanger, *Being-in-the-World: Selected Papers of Ludwig Binswanger*, trans. J. Needham (New York: Harper, 1968, c1963), p. 158.
21. SE VII, *Three Essays*, p. 163.
22. Ibid., p. 163.

Introduction to Part II

1. Cf. Marjorie Grene, *Approaches to a Philosophical Biology* (New York: Basic Books, 1965).
2. The opening to a new ground realized by psychoanalysis has not gone unnoticed in the philosophical movements of our century. In the work of Merleau-Ponty, to name only one prominent instance, we find an explicit attempt to clarify phenomenologically the fact of being embodied as the basis of mind. This attempt led Merleau-Ponty to a rendering of embodied being as a reality that escapes conceptual elucidation within the alternatives provided by the dualistic framework of understanding. "The perceiving mind is an incarnated mind," he writes in a posthumously published prospectus of his work.

> I have tried, first of all, to re-establish the roots of the mind in its body and in its world, going against doctrines which treat perception as a simple result of the action of external things on our body as well as those which insist on the autonomy of consciousness. These philosophies commonly forget—in favor of a pure exteriority or of a pure interiority—the insertion of mind in corporeality, the ambiguous relation which we entertain with our body and, correlatively, with perceived things.

The quote may be found in Maurice Merleau-Ponty, *The Primacy of Perception*, ed. James M. Edie (Evanston: Northwestern University Press, 1964), p. 4.
3. *The Origins of Psychoanalysis*, letter 96, p. 264; editor's interpolation.
4. *The Freud/Jung Letters: The Correspondence between Sigmund Freud and C. G. Jung*, ed. William McGuire, Bollingen Series XCIV (Princeton: Princeton University Press, 1974), letter 288F, p. 472.

Chapter 5

1. Cf. Martin Heidegger, *Being and Time*, trans. J. MacQuarrie and E. Robinson (New York: Harper & Row, 1967), sec. I.5.B, pp. 210–24.
2. SE XV, *Introductory Lectures*, p. 239.
3. G. W. F. Hegel, *The Phenomenology of Mind*, trans. J. B. Baillie (New York: Harper, 1967), p. 83.
4. SE V, *Interpretation*, p. 603.
5. Hegel, *Phenomenology*, p. 87.
6. SE XXIII, *Outline*, pp. 144 and 157 respectively; cf. also SE I, "Project," p. 307, for a less self-clarified articulation of the same meaning.
7. *Letters of Sigmund Freud*, letter 237, Dec. 9, 1928, p. 384.
8. SE V, p. 378.
9. Ibid., pp. 35–36.
10. Ricoeur, *Freud and Philosophy*, p. 6.
11. SE IV, p. 1.
12. SE V, p. 507.
13. Ibid., p. 565.
14. SE IV, p. 101.
15. Ibid., p. 101.
16. Ibid., p. 121.
17. SE V, pp. 510–11.

Chapter 6

1. SE Iv, p. 63.
2. SE XIV, "On the History of the Psychoanalytic Movement," p. 22.
3. *Origins of Psychoanalysis*, letter 39, Jan. 1, 1896, p. 141.
4. Ibid., letter 44, April 2, 1896, p. 162.
5. SE IV, pp. 41–42. While I have rearranged the sequence of the points Freud makes in this passage in order to highlight those relevant to my argument, I have not, I think, violated thereby either the spirit or the letter of Freud's views as he conveys them there.
6. SE VI, *The Psychopathology of Everyday Life*, pp. 258–59.
7. Cf. *Logical Positivism*, ed. A. J. Ayer (New York: Free Press, 1959), particularly Rudolf Carnap's "The Elimination of Metaphysics through the Logical Analysis of Language," pp. 60–81.
8. *Letters of Sigmund Freud*, letter 228, p. 376.
9. Hegel, *Phenomenology*, p. 86.
10. SE XIII, p. 161.
11. Immanuel Kant, *Critique of Pure Reason*, trans. Norman Kemp Smith (Toronto: Macmillan, 1965), p. 56.
12. Cf. *Letters of Sigmund Freud*, letter 176, p. 323; see also chap. 4, n. 13, above.
13. SE XV, *Introductory Lectures*, p. 22.

14. Martin Heidegger, *Hegel's Concept of Experience* (New York: Harper & Row, 1970), p. 144.

15. Hegel, p. 144.

16. Ibid., p. 145.

17. Ibid., p. 80.

18. Karl Marx, *Economic and Philosophic Manuscripts of 1844,* 4th ed. rev. (Moscow: Progress Publishers, 1974), p. 97.

19. It should be noted, however, that natural science has had no little difficulty in knowing what to do with the spoils of its victory. These difficulties are patent in the various scientific speculations on how "consciousness" evolved by a process of natural selection. What such efforts usually forget is that the efficacy of a mechanistic causal scheme such as Darwin's is underwritten by an ontological imperative that eliminates from the outset consciousness (awareness, purpose, intention, volition) as irrelevant to the phenomena to be explained. Cf. Karl Popper, "Scientific Reduction and the Essential Incompleteness of all Science," in Jose Ayala and Theodosius Dobzhansky, eds., *Studies in the Philosophy of Biology* (Berkeley: University of California Press, 1974), p. 272.

20. Aristotle, *Metaphysics,* Book Beta, 999b:5–7, trans. Richard Hope (Ann Arbor: University of Michigan Press, 1960), p. 51.

21. Jonas, *The Phenomenon of Life,* pp. 47–48.

22. Ibid., p. 40n.

23. In Milič Čapek, *The Philosophical Impact of Contemporary Physics* (New York: Van Nostrand, 1961), p. 122.

24. Ibid., p. 121.

25. Jonas, p. 38.

26. Ibid., p. 40.

27. Cf. Immanuel Kant, *Critique of Judgement,* trans. J. H. Bernard (New York: Hafner Publishing, 1972), sec. 75, p. 248.

28. Dewey, "The Influence of Darwin," pp. 1, 5.

29. Čapek, p. 124.

30. Ibid., p. 96.

31. Darwin, p. 456.

32. Jacob, *The Logic of Life,* p. 296.

33. Cf. Darwin, pp. 27–28; see also the introduction by William Coleman to *The Interpretation of Animal Form,* ed. W. Coleman (New York: Johnson Reprint Corp., 1967). The book is a collection of classical essays on morphology, in reprint.

34. Haeckel quoted in E. S. Russell, *Form and Function: A Contribution to the History of Animal Morphology* (London: John Murray, 1916), p. 253.

35. Charles Coulton Gillispie, *The Edge of Objectivity* (Princeton: Princeton University Press, 1960), p. 317.

36. Dewey, p. 4.

37. Darwin quoted in Jane Oppenheimer, "An Embryological Enigma in the *Origin of Species,*" in *Forerunners of Darwin,* ed. Bently Glass,

Owsei Temkin, and William L. Straus, Jr. (Baltimore: Johns Hopkins University Press, 1959), p. 292.

38. SE XI, *Leonardo da Vinci*, p. 97.

Chapter 7

1. Friedrich Nietzsche, *Beyond Good and Evil*, trans. Walter Kaufmann (New York: Vintage Books, 1967), p. 161.

2. Aristotle, Book Alpha the Less, 993b:28–32, p. 36.

3. SE XI, *Leonardo da Vinci*, p. 136.

4. The Leonardo study has been severely criticized. Freud had relatively little biographical information available to him concerning Leonardo. But, more importantly, his interpretation is based upon a mistranslation of Leonardo's childhood memory, which constitutes its central piece of evidence. Cf. Paul Roazen, *Freud: Political and Social Thought* (new York: Vintage Books, 1968), pp. 114–15. The very poverty of interpretative material, however, combined with the fact that the study deals with a *completed* life, lends a simplicity and clarity to it that bring the psychoanalytic view of life sharply into focus. In our exposition we shall further simplify Freud's argument in order to concentrate upon the principles underlying his analysis.

5. SE XI, p. 135.

6. SE VII, *Three Essays*, p. 239.

7. Ibid., p. 234.

8. *Letters of Sigmund Freud,* letter 149, p. 293.

9. SE XI, pp. 80–81.

10. Ibid., p. 137.

11. Ibid.

12. SE XIV, "The Unconscious," p. 187.

13. Alfred North Whitehead, *Process and Reality* (New York: Macmillan, 1927), p. 106. Whitehead's inverted Kantianism provides a key, I think, to the difficult question of Freud's relation to Kant. As mentioned in Chap. 3, n. 20, above, Freud's library contained a copy of Kant's *Critique of Pure Reason*, signed by Freud and dated 1882. Moreover, Kant is the philosopher most often alluded to in Freud's writings. A review of Freud's references to Kant, however, reveals a certain crudity of understanding on Freud's part as to the purport of Kant's critical philosophy. Nonetheless, my guess—and on this question guesses are probably the best we can do— is that a serious but fruitful misunderstanding of Kant's "Transcendental Aesthetic" may have been crucial to Freud in clarifying the problematic which the grounding operation was designed to resolve. The point here is Freud's *inversion* of Kant along the lines indicated by Whitehead's philosophy of organism.

This inversion also takes another form in Freud. What for Freud lies beyond the bounds of sense is not Kant's noumenal realm, but the body itself as it gives rise within to the appearances of consciousness. From his visit to Freud in 1910, Ludwig Binswanger reports Freud's belief that "just as Kant postulated the thing in itself behind the phenomenal world, so he himself postulated the unconscious being the conscious that is accessible to our experience, but that can never be directly experienced" (Ludwig Binswanger, "My First Three Visits with Freud in Vienna," in *Freud, We Knew Him,* ed. Hendrik M. Ruitenbeck [Detroit, 1973], pp. 366–67). Related to this is Freud's discussion in the 1915 edition of the *Three Essays* of the roles of "constitutional" and "accidental" factors in the individual's psychosexual development. "The constitutional factor must await experiences before it can make itself felt; the accidental factor must have a constitutional factor in order to come into operation" (SE VII, p. 239). The Kantian provenance of this formulation becomes patent in the allusion to Kant's schematism found in "An Infantile Neurosis," where Freud equates "the categories of philosophy" with "the phylogenetically inherited schemata," which "are concerned with the business of 'placing' the impressions derived from actual experience" (SE XVII, p. 119). For an illuminating discussion of the issues raised by this dimension of Freud's thought, though without relation to Freudianism itself, cf. Konrad Lorenz, "Kant's Doctrine of the A Priori in the Light of Contemporary Biology," in Richard I. Evans, *Konrad Lorenz: The Man and His Ideas* (New York, 1975), pp. 181–217.

Finally, in an odd, posthumously published note written at the end of his life, Freud indicates an awareness that he had inverted Kant. "Space may be the projection of the extension of the psychical apparatus. No other derivation is probable. Instead of Kant's *a priori* determinants of our psychical apparatus. Psyche is extended; knows nothing about it" (SE XXIII, "Findings, Ideas, Problems," p. 300).

14. SEE XIX, "Negation," pp. 237–38.
15. SE V, *Interpretation,* pp. 565–66.
16. Ibid., p. 566.
17. SE XVI, *Introductory Lectures,* p. 372.
18. SE V, p. 620.
19. SE XIV, "Instincts and Their Vicissitudes," p. 119.
20. Ibid., pp. 133–34.

Chapter 8

1. Friedrich Nietzsche, *The Birth of Tragedy,* trans. Walter Kaufmann (New York: Vintage Books, 1967), pp. 95–98 passim.
2. Ibid., p. 96.
3. SE XXII, "Why War?" pp. 203 and 213.
4. Ibid., p. 211.
5. SE XXII, *New Introductory Lectures,* p. 95.
6. Jones, *Sigmund Freud,* vol. 3, p. 287.
7. Herbert Marcuse, *Eros and Civilization* (New York: Vintage Books, 1962), pp. 217–51.

8. SE VII, *Three Essays*, 6th ed., p. 168, n. 2.
9. Marcuse, p. 97.
10. Jones, vol. 3, p. 44; the quote is from an early letter by Freud (Aug. 16, 1882). Freud's identification of the psychoanalytic instincts with Schopenhauer's will is found in SE XVII, "A Difficulty in the Path of Psychoanalysis, pp. 143–44.
11. *Letters of Sigmund Freud*, letter 172, May 25, 1916, p. 318.
12. SE XII, "Formulations on the Two Principles of Mental Functioning," p. 218.
13. Ibid., pp. 219 and 218.
14. Ibid., p. 219.
15. Ibid., pp. 219–20; 220–21 passim; 222.
16. Ibid., p. 219, n. 4.
17. Ibid., p. 222.
18. Ibid., p. 223.
19. SE VII, *Three Essays*, p. 234.
20. SE XI, "The Psychoanalytic View of a Psychogenic Disturbance of Vision," p. 215.

Chapter 9

1. Marcuse, *Eros and Civilization*, p. 31.
2. Ibid., pp. 31–32.
3. Ibid., p. 32.
4. Ibid.
5. Ibid.
6. It must be added here, however, that the argument of *Eros and Civilization* is seriously flawed by Marcuse's misunderstanding of the reality principle. Marcuse identifies the reality principle with the forces of repression. This identification is simply wrong. The reality principle, to be sure, imposes restrictions upon impulse. But these restrictions are not repressions. They are consciously made calculative adjustments of internal demands to external possibilities of satisfaction. The reality principle *safeguards* the pleasure principle by exchanging a "momentary pleasure, uncertain in its results" for "an assured pleasure at a later time" along "a new path." The logic of adaptation that informs the reality principle bears no relation to the restrictions upon impulse imposed by repression. In essence, the reality principle is a scientific norm—an appropriation of the biological concept of adaptation as the psychoanalytic criterion for distinguishing normal from abnormal mental processes. But it is also a norm in the ethical sense—a standard for adjudicating our relationships in the waking world of everyday existence. If the core of our being is to be sought in the darkness within, the reality principle nonetheless chastens us to accept the limited possibilities for self-realization in the world without.

The place of repression in relation to the two principles of mental functioning is in fact the opposite of what Marcuse would lead us to believe. Repression stands on the side, not of the reality principle, but of the pleasure principle. In speaking of the "older, primary processes," Freud tells us that their "governing purpose is easy to recognize; it is described as the pleasure-unpleasure principle or more simply, the pleasure principle. These processes strive towards pleasure; psychical activity draws back from any event which might arouse unpleasure." He then adds parenthetically, "(Here we have repression.)" (SE XII, p. 219). By contrast, one of the adaptations necessitated by the reality principle is an "impartial passing of judgement" which *takes the place of repression*. In fact, Freud is at pains in the "Formulations" to avoid the problem of repression, which he could handle only at the phylogenetic level—that is, by writing *Totem and Taboo*. Repression arises from a conflict within desire indicated by the two sides of the pleasure principle—that is, the striving for pleasure, on the one hand, and the avoidance of unpleasure, on the other.

7. SE XII, "Formulations," p. 223.
8. Ibid.
9. SE XIII, *Totem and Taboo*, p. 74.
10. *Letters of Sigmund Freud*, letter 169, p. 315.
11. SE XIII, *Totem and Taboo*, p. 88.
12. SE XXII, *New Introductory Lectures*, pp. 158–59.
13. Ibid., p. 170.
14. SE XIII, "Scientific Interest," p. 186.
15. The notion that science, *qua* technology, is the organ of man's instrumental adaptation to nature has its roots in Darwinism. Marx was among the first to articulate the logic of this connection. In a famous footnote to the first volume of *Capital*, we read:

> Darwin has interested us in the history of Nature's Technology, i.e., in the formation of the organs of plants and animals, which organs serve as the instruments of production for sustaining life. Does not the history of the productive organs of man, of organs that are the material basis of all social organization, deserve equal attention? And would not such a history be easier to compile because, as Vico says, human history differs from natural history in this, that we have made the former but not the latter? Technology discloses man's mode of dealing with Nature, the processes of production by which he sustains his life, and thereby also lays bare the mode of formation of his social relations, and of the mental conceptions that flow from them. [New York: International Publishers, 1967, p. 372, n. 3]

For very different reasons, both Freud and Marx manage to avoid the reduction of the human life-world to the level of biological necessity, which Marx's conflation of nature's "technology" and man's "organs of production" portends. Freud avoids this conflation because his starting point is with the biological needs of the human organism, not as they appear from without in man's "metabolism with nature," as Marx once put it, but as they are manifest from within in the form of wish, impulse, and desire. Thus, as Freud explains in the summary of *Totem and Taboo* referred to in n. 14, psychoanalysis starts out from the basic idea that the principal function of the mental mechanism is to relieve the tensions created in him by his needs. One part of this task can be achieved by extracting satisfaction from the external world; and for this purpose it is essential to have control over the real world. But the satisfaction of another part of these needs—among them certain affective impulses—is regularly frustrated by reality. This leads to the further task of finding some other means of dealing with the unsatisfied impulses. The whole course of civilization is no more than an account of the various methods adopted by mankind of "binding" their unsatisfied wishes, which, according to changing conditions (modified, moreover, by technological advances) have been met by reality sometimes with favor and sometimes with frustration. [SE XIII, "The Claims of Psychoanalysis to Scientific Interest," p. 186]

It is telling that in *Totem and Taboo* Freud identifies the phylogenetic provenance of technology not with primitive man's tool-making capacity but with a will to control the external world manifest in the meaning structures of the prescientific life-world that go under the title of magic. Magic arises because the wishes of the "adult primitive man . . . are accompanied by a motor impulse, *the will, which is later destined to alter the whole face of the earth in order to satisfy his wishes*" (my italics) (SE XIII, p. 84).

16. SE XIII, *Totem and Taboo*, p. 90.

17. I must defend myself here against the charge that I have overlooked Freud's employment of the concept of narcissism in the Schreber case, "Psycho-analytic Notes on an Autobiographical Account of a Case of Paranoia *(Dementia Paranoides)*" (1911), which he wrote a year before composing the first essay of *Totem and Taboo*. My defense is a simple one. Freud began his research for *Totem and Taboo* in 1910, around the time he wrote to Jung that he was becoming increasingly convinced of the "cultural value" of psychoanalysis (cf. *Freud/Jung Letters*, ed. William McGuire [Princeton: Princeton University Press, 1974], letter 201F, July 5, 1910, p. 240). Paranoia was the pathology of projected meaning par excellence which Freud had already cited in 1901 as the analogy for mythical and religious phenomena. Indeed, paranoia was prominent among the psychopathological phenomena Freud investigated during the prepsychoanalytic period. But, after 1899, "scarcely a mention of paranoia [is to be found] in Freud's published writings" until the Schreber case (editor's note, SE XII, p. 4). The Schreber case was composed in conjunction with the "Formulations" after the epistle to Jung of July 1910, when the task of addressing the question of culture came to the forefront of Freud's concerns. That is to say, Freud finally undertook the long-deferred analysis of paranoia for the purpose of executing the task of *Totem and Taboo*—of engaging in the psychoanalytic interpretation of the phenomena of culture. In a postscript to the Schreber case, written in the fall of 1911, Freud first announces his imminent venture into the anthropological dimension (SE XII, pp. 80–82). Cf. Jones, vol. 2, pp. 392–404 passim.

18. SE XIII, *Totem and Taboo*, pp. 88–89.
19. Ibid., pp. 91–92.

Chapter 10

1. SE XIV, "On Narcissism," p. 75.
2. Ibid., p. 76.
3. Ibid., p. 76.
4. Ibid., p. 78.
5. Ibid., p. 79.
6. Ibid., p. 79.
7. Between the publication of "On Narcissism" (1914) and *Beyond the Pleasure Principle* (1920) lies an intriguing episode related to the emergence of Freud's instinct theory. Unfortunately, this episode has been shrouded in obscurity owing to the disturbing circumstance that the last major Freud correspondence—with Sandor Ferenczi—remains to this date unpublished. The episode turns on Ferenczi's "bioanalytic" speculations, published in 1924 under the title *Versuch einer Genitaltheorie* and in English translation as *Thalassa: A Theory of Genitality* (New York: W.W. Norton, 1968). The theories developed in this book, Ferenczi informs us, first crystallized at the beginning of the Great War. In 1915 and again in 1919 Ferenczi presented them to Freud, who encouraged him on both occasions to prepare his ideas for publication. Writing to Karl Abraham on November 11, 1917, Freud makes clear reference to Ferenczi's speculations in terms of a "Lamarck idea."

> It arose between Ferenczi and me, but neither of us has the time or spirit to tackle it at present. The idea is to put Lamarck entirely on our own ground and to show that the 'necessity' that according to him creates and transforms organs is nothing but the power of unconscious ideas over one's own body, of which we see remnants in hysteria, in short the 'omnipotence of thoughts'. This would actually supply an explanation of adaptation; it would put the coping stone on psycho-analysis. There would be two linked principles of progressive change, adaptation of one's own body and subsequent transformation of the external world (autoplasticity and heteroplasticity), etc. [*A Psychoanalytic Dialogue: The Letters of Sigmund Freud and Karl Abraham 1907–1926*, pp. 261–62]

We find a passing reference to the same project a few months earlier in a letter to Georg Groddeck of June 6, 1917. The "Ucs exerts on somatic processes an influence of far greater plastic power than the conscious ever can," he informs Groddeck. "The same point of view, moreover, has caused [Ferenczi] to make for me a biological experiment to show how a consistent continuation of Lamarck's theory of evolution coincides with the final outcome of psychoanalytic thinking" (*Letters of Sigmund Freud*, no. 176, p. 323).

Freud's newfound readiness to apply psychoanalytic findings to biological phenomena, which came to fruition in *Beyond the Pleasure Principle*, is already at work in these daring formulations. In a published reference to

Ferenczi's *Versuch einer Genitaltheorie* shortly after the book appeared, however, Freud is far more cautious. Always mindful of the sometimes conflicting claims of private conviction and what could be defended in the realm of public scientific discourse, Freud characterized Ferenczi's book in a 1924 footnote to the *Three Essays* as "a work which, though somewhat fanciful, is nevertheless of the greatest interest" (SE VII, p. 229, n. 2). He is somewhat more expansive in the eulogy he wrote in 1933 on the occasion of Ferenczi's death. There Freud calls the book "a biological rather than a psychoanalytic study" which, nonetheless, constitutes "the boldest application of psychoanalysis that was ever attempted." Again, however, Freud qualifies his praise by noting the need, as yet premature, "to distinguish what can be accepted as an authentic discovery from what seeks, in the fashion of scientific phantasy, to guess at future knowledge" (SE XXII, p. 228). We may conjecture that Freud's public posture was dictated by prudential considerations. To identify psychoanalysis with a general theory of evolution—and an unorthodox one at that—would be reaching too far and would have needlessly exposed psychoanalysis to criticisms Freud was in no position to counter.

No doubt the letters of Freud and Ferenczi would tell us much about this and other matters during the period of the Great War. They might also help to fill another major gap in our understanding of Freud's development. In 1915 Freud set out "to provide a stable theoretical foundation for psychoanalysis" by writing a series of "Papers on Metapsychology." He later abandoned this project, however, publishing five of the papers separately and apparently destroying seven others (SE XIV, pp. 105–07). How Freud's decision to abandon this projected consummation of psychoanalytic theory relates to his encounter with the limitations of his original theoretical framework analyzed above would be interesting to know. Significantly, one of the missing or destroyed papers was on "Consciousness," and another on "Projection" or "Paranoia"—two areas in which the limitations necessitating the introduction of the concept of narcissism must have become increasingly vivid. Did Freud confide in Ferenczi about such difficulties? The answer must await the belated publication of their letters.

8. SE XVIII, *Beyond the Pleasure Principle*, p. 24.
9. Ibid., p. 60.
10. Ibid., p. 49.
11. Ibid., p. 30.
12. Ibid., pp. 60–61, n. 1.
13. Ibid., p. 36.
14. Ibid., pp. 38–39.
15. Ibid., p. 50.
16. Ibid., p. 55.
17. Cf. chap. 9, n. 17, above.
18. SE XII, "Psychoanalytic Notes," p. 71.
19. Ibid., p. 71.
20. Ibid., p. 49.
21. Ibid., p. 71.

22. SE XVIII, *Group Psychology and the Analysis of the Ego*, p. 130.
23. SE XIX, *The Ego and the Id*, p. 46.
24. SE XVIII, *Beyond the Pleasure Principle*, pp. 57–58.

Chapter 11

1. SE XX, *An Autobiographical Study*, pp. 71–72.
2. Ibid., p. 72. What these reflections obscure is the status of the two further contributions to psychoanalysis Freud makes in his final period. The theory of the instincts and the psychology of the ego and its dependent relations are clearly integral to the cultural concerns dominating that final period. For only *after* solving the problem of the origins of religion and morality in *Totem and Taboo* does Freud develop his theory of the dynamic conflicts of the ego, the id, and the superego—conflicts that in 1935 he sees the events of human history to be repetitions of. That is to say, Freud's final theory of mental life is governed by his interest in the solution of "cultural problems" and grows out of a concern to provide a psychodynamic basis for the cultural phenomena that are manifest upon the wider stage of history.
3. SE VI, *The Psychopathology of Everyday Life*, pp. 258–59. Cf. my earlier discussion of this passage on pp. 78–80, above.
4. SE XX, *An Autobiographical Study*, p. 8.
5. G. G. Simpson, *Biology and Man* (New York: Harcourt Brace Jovanovich, 1969), p. 80.
6. *Letters of Sigmund Freud*, letter 7, p. 38. Freud places these words in the mouth of an "old Jew." Cf. John M. Cuddihy, *The Ordeal of Civility* (New York: Basic Books, 1974), for a grossly reductionistic and overstated, but nonetheless provocative, analysis of Freud's thought in terms of his position in European society as a secularized Jew. See also Freud's letter to Oskar Pfister in which Freud asks why it was left to a "completely godless Jew" to discover psychoanalysis (*Psychoanalysis and Faith: The Letters of Sigmund Freud and Oskar Pfister* [New York: Basic Books, 1963], p. 63).
7. Jones, vol. 3, p. 495.
8. SE VI, *Everyday Life*, pp. 257–58.
9. *The Portable Nietzsche*, ed. and trans. Walter Kaufmann (Middlesex: Penguin Books, 1976), p. 486.
10. E. A. Burtt, *The Metaphysical Foundations*, p. 234.
11. Ibid.
12. SE V, *Interpretation*, p. 536.
13. SE XIX, *The Ego and the Id*, p. 18.
14. SE XXI, *Civilization and Its Discontents*, p. 122.
15. SE XIII, *Totem and Taboo*, p. 64.
16. Ibid., p. 85.
17. SE XVIII, *Group Psychology*, p. 130.
18. *Freud/Jung Letters*, letter 201F, July 5, 1910, p. 340.
19. SE XII, pp. 70–71.

Bibliography

Correspondence

Abraham, Hilda, and Freud, Ernst L., eds. *A Psychoanalytic Dialogue: The Letters of Sigmund Freud and Karl Abraham.* New York: Basic Books, 1965.

Bonaparte, Marie; Freud, Anna; and Kris, Ernst, eds. *The Origins of Psychoanalysis, Letters to Wilhelm Fleiss, Drafts and Notes: 1887–1902.* New York: Basic Books, 1954.

Freud, Ernst L. *The Letters of Sigmund Freud, 1873–1939.* London: Hogarth Press, 1970.

McGuire, William, ed. *The Freud/Jung Letters: The Correspondence between Sigmund Freud and C. G. Jung.* Bollingen Series XCIV. Princeton: Princeton University Press, 1970.

Meng, Heinrich, and Freud, Ernst L., eds. *Psychoanalysis and Faith: The Letters of Sigmund Freud and Oskar Pfister.* New York: Basic Books, 1963.

Pfeiffer, Ernst, ed. *Sigmund Freud and Lou Andreas-Salomé: Letters.* New York: Harcourt Brace Jovanovich, 1972.

Books

Allen, Garland. *Life Science in the Twentieth Century.* New York: Wiley, 1975.

Arendt, Hannah. *Between Past and Future.* New York: Viking Press, 1961.
———. *The Human Condition.* Garden City: Doubleday, 1958.

Aristotle, *Metaphysics.* Translated by Richard Hope. Ann Arbor: University of Michigan Press, 1960.

Ayala, Jose F., and Dobzhansky, Theodosius. *Studies in the Philosophy of Biology.* Berkeley: University of California Press, 1974.

Bacon, Francis. *The New Organon.* Edited by Fulton H. Anderson. Indianapolis: Bobbs-Merrill, 1960.

Binswanger, Ludwig. *Being-in-the-World: Selected Papers of Ludwig Binswanger*. Edited by Jacob Needham. New York: Harper Torchbooks, 1968.

Bleibtreu, Hermann K., comp. *Evolutionary Anthropology*. Boston: Allyn & Bacon, 1969.

Burtt, E. A. *The Metaphysical Foundations of Modern Science*. Rev. ed. Garden City: Doubleday, 1954.

Čapek, Milič. *The Philosophical Impact of Contemporary Physics*. New York: Van Nostrand, 1961.

Cassirer, Ernst. *The Philosophy of the Enlightenment*. Translated by Fritz C. A. Koelin and James A. Pettegrove. Boston: Beacon Press, 1955.

Collingwood, R. G. *The Idea of Nature*. London: Oxford University Press, 1960.

Comte, Auguste. *Introduction to Positive Philosophy*. Edited, with a revised translation, by Frederick Ferre. Indianapolis: Bobbs-Merrill, 1970.

Darwin, Charles. *The Descent of Man, and Selection of Relation to Sex*. London: John Murray, 1871.

———. *The Expression of Emotions in Man and Animals*. London: John Murray, 1872.

———. *The Origin of Species by Means of Natural Selection*. First edition. Middlesex: Penguin, 1968.

Descartes, Rene. *The Philosophical Works of Descartes*. Translated by Elizabeth S. Haldane and G. R. T. Ross. 2 vols. Cambridge: Cambridge University Press, 1972.

Dilthey, Wilhelm. *Pattern and Meaning in History*. Translated and edited by H. P. Rickman. New York: Harper & Row, 1961.

Eiseley, Loren. *Darwin's Century*. Garden City: Doubleday, 1961.

Fancher, Raymond E. *Psychoanalytic Psychology: The Development of Freud's Thought*. New York: W. W. Norton, 1973.

Fechner, Gustav A. *Elements of Psychophysics*. Edited by Edwin G. Boring. New York: Holt, Rinehart, and Winston, 1966.

Ferenczi, Sandor. *Thalassa: A Theory of Genitality*. New York: W. W. Norton, 1968.

Freud, Sigmund. *The Standard Edition of the Complete Psychological Works of Sigmund Freud*. Edited by James Strachey. 24 vols. London: Hogarth Press, 1953–74.

Galilei, Galileo. *Dialogue concerning the Two Chief World Systems*. 2d ed. Translated by Stillman Drake. Berkeley: University of California Press, 1967.

Ghilesin, Michael T. *The Triumph of the Darwinian Method*. Berkeley: University of California Press, 1969.

Gillispie, Charles Coulston. *The Edge of Objectivity*. Princeton: Princeton University Press, 1960.

Glass, Bently; Temkin, Owsei; and Straus, William L., Jr., eds. *Forerunners of Darwin: 1745–1859.* Baltimore: Johns Hopkins University Press, 1959.

Glick, Thomas F., ed. *The Comparative Reception of Darwinism.* Austin: University of Texas Press, 1972.

Goudge, T. A. *The Ascent of Life.* Toronto: University of Toronto Press, 1961.

Greene, John C. *The Death of Adam.* Ames: Iowa State University Press, 1959.

Grene, Marjorie. *Approaches to a Philosophical Biology.* New York: Basic Books, 1965.

Habermas, Jürgen. *Knowledge and Human Interests.* Translated by Jeremy J. Shapiro. Boston: Beacon Press, 1971.

Haeckel, Ernst. *The Riddle of the Universe at the Close of the Nineteenth Century.* Translated by Joseph McCabe. New York: Harper, 1900.

Hegel, G. W. F. *The Phenomenology of Mind.* Translated by J. B. Baillie. New York: Harper & Row, 1967.

Heidegger, Martin. *Being and Time.* Translated by J. MacQuarrie and E. Robinson. New York: Harper & Row, 1967.

———. *Hegel's Concept of Experience.* New York: Harper & Row, 1970.

———. *Kant and the Problem of Metaphysics.* Translated by James A. Churchill. Bloomington: Indiana University Press, 1962.

Hodges, Herbert A. *The Philosophy of Wihelm Dilthey.* London: Routledge & Kegan Paul, 1952.

Husserl, Edmund. *Ideas.* Translated by W. R. Boyce Gibson. London: Collier-Macmillan, 1962.

Jacob, François. *The Logic of Life.* Translated by Betty E. Spillman. New York: Vintage Books, 1976.

Jonas, Hans. *The Phenomenon of Life.* New York: Delta, 1966.

———. *Philosophical Essays: From Ancient Creed to Technological Man.* Englewood Cliffs, N.J.: Prentice-Hall, 1974.

Jones, Ernest. *Sigmund Freud: Life and Work.* 3 vols. London: Hogarth Press, 1957.

Jung, Carl G. *The Collected Works of C. G. Jung.* Bollingen Series XX. Vols. 3 and 4. New York: Pantheon Books. 1960, 1961.

Kant, Immanuel. *Critique of Judgement.* Translated by J. H. Bernard. New York: Hafner, 1972.

———. *Critique of Pure Reason.* Translated by Normal Kemp Smith. New York: St. Martin's Press, 1965.

Lacan, Jacques. *The Function of Language in Psychoanalysis.* In *The Language of the Self.* Translated by Anthony Wilden. Baltimore: Johns Hopkins University Press, 1968.

Lazlo, Ervin. *The Systems View of the World.* New York: George Braziller, 1972.

Leibniz, Gottfried Wilhelm von. *Monadology and Other Philosophical Essays*. Translated by Paul Schrecker and Anne Martin Schrecker. Indianapolis: Bobbs-Merrill, 1965.

Marcuse, Herbert. *Eros and Civilization*. New York: Vintage Books, 1962.

Marx, Karl. *Capital*. Vol. 1. Translated by Samuel Moore and Edward Aveling. Edited by Frederick Engels. New York: International Publishers, 1967.

——. *Economic Philosophic Manuscripts of 1844*. 4th rev. ed. Translated by Martin Milligan. Moscow: Progress Publishers, 1974.

Merleau-Ponty, Maurice. *The Primacy of Perception and Other Essays*. Edited by James M. Edie. Evanston: Northwestern University Press, 1964.

Newton, Isaac. *Newton's Philosophy of Nature: Selections from His Writings*. Edited by H. S. Thayer. New York: Hafner Press, 1953.

Nietzsche, Friedrich. *Beyond Good and Evil*. New York: Vintage Books, 1966.

——. *The Birth of Tragedy*. New York: Vintage Books, 1966.

——. *The Will to Power*. New York: Vintage Books, 1967.

Ortega y Gasset, José. *History as a System*. New York: W. W. Norton, 1961.

Ricoeur, Paul. *Freud and Philosophy*. New Haven: Yale University Press, 1970.

Rieff, Philip. *Freud: The Mind of the Moralist*. Garden City: Doubleday, 1961.

Roazen, Paul. *Freud: Political and Social Thought*. New York: Vintage Books, 1968.

Robinson, Paul A. *The Freudian Left*. New York: Harper & Row, 1969.

Russell, E. S. *Form and Function*. London: John Murray, 1916.

Schmidt, Alfred. *The Concept of Nature in Marx*. Translated by Ben Fowkes.

Simpson, George Gaylord. *Biology and Man*. New York: Harcourt Brace Jovanovich, 1969.

——. *The Meaning of Evolution*. Rev. ed. New Haven: Yale University Press, 1967.

Spicker, Stuart F., ed. *The Philosophy of the Body*. Chicago: Quadrangle Books, 1970.

Weber, Max. *From Max Weber: Essays in Sociology*. Edited by H. H. Gerth and C. Wright Mills. New York: Oxford University Press, 1946.

Index

Adaptation, 59, 91–92, 113–14, 115, 165n
Andreas-Salomé, Lou, 111
Animism, 123, 127, 128–29
Appearances, 111–12, 144–46
Arendt, Hannah, 8
Aristophanes, 138
Aristotle, 3, 83, 88, 92, 101; his *Metaphysics*, 85, 96

Bacon, Francis, 125
Being, and becoming, 92–93, 96
Bioanalysis, 168–69n
Biogenetic law, 90–94, 123, 126–27
Biological hypothesis, 53, 56, 58, 62, 109, 110, 115, 116, 121, 148
Body: as ground, 21, 22, 26–27, 39, 40, 48, 54, 160n; existential primacy of, 21, 30
Breuer, Joseph, 19, 32, 35
Burtt, E. A., 23

Čapek, Milič, 87, 88
Cartesian cogito, 27–28
Cartesian dualism, 3, 7, 23, 24–26, 56, 84, 102; as framework of understanding, 23, 24, 26–27, 28, 32, 40, 54. *See also* Descartes
Catharsis, theory of, 33, 48
Cathartic method, 32
Comte, Auguste, 126
Consciousness: epistemological role of, 11, 18, 19, 20, 22, 23, 56; in relation to

unconscious, 11, 35–38, 114; and metaphysics, 83–84; and natural selection, 162n
Copernican revolution, 16, 70, 76, 77, 84, 86
Copernicus, Nicolaus, 83, 111, 125

Daimon, Freud's, 3, 82
Darwin, Charles, 1, 82, 125, 134, 137, 142, 149, 150; his *Origin of Species*, 16, 17, 58, 84, 89, 91. *See also* Darwinism
Darwinism: Freud's relation to, 3, 16–19, 65, 69, 100, 103, 142–43, 149–51; psychology of, 17, 18, 19; mechanisms of, 58–59, 86, 89; philosophical implications of, 77, 80, 85–87, 89–94
Descartes, René, 1, 83
Dewey, John, 16, 88, 92
Dilthey, Wilhelm, 1, 44–47, 49, 57, 122
Dreams, 10, 38, 70, 72–75, 111

Ego: Freud's notion of, 10, 43, 44, 48–49, 67, 121, 130, 131, 139; thinking, 27, 32, 65; deferred investigation of, 33, 40; teleology of, 33, 47; occlusion of, 33–34, 44, 53, 145; unity of, 35, 36, 41, 49; psychology of, 38, 48–49, 121, 151, 170n; sovereignty of, 40, 43; in Dilthey, 46–47; narcissism of, 47, 48–49, 131–32
Einstein, Albert, 107–08

175

Aristotle; Descartes; Hegel; Kant;
    Philosophy
Metapsychology, 2, 3, 12, 13, 14, 29–30;
    and biology, 14, 30, 48, 50, 66. *See
    also* Metaphysics, and meta-
    psychology
Michelangelo, 4
Mind, epistemological priority of, 21, 30
Mind–body problem, 20–21, 54
Mythology, 79, 107–10 passim, 118–19,
    131, 138, 147

Narcissism, 47, 49, 128, 147; concept of,
    67, 127–28, 130, 131, 149, 167n; basis
    for Eros and death instincts, 133–38
    passim
Natural science, 1, 2, 24–26, 79, 107–09,
    112
Newton, Sir Isaac, 86, 88, 89, 125, 145,
    146
Newtonian-Laplacean cosmology, 86,
    87, 88
Nietzsche, Friedrich, 1, 2, 95, 107, 108,
    110, 144–45

Ontogeny. *See* Biogenetic law

Paranoia, 135–36, 137
Philosophy, 1, 2, 71, 77, 82, 83, 150–51.
    See also Metaphysics
Phylogeny. *See* Biogenetic law
Plato, 83, 111, 138
Pleasure principle, 112–15 passim, 118,
    119, 122, 126–27, 129
Psychoanalytic: theory transformed, 3,
    66, 130–31, 147; discourse, 7–8,
    13–15; dialogue, 8–11, 34–35, 48;
    field of observation, 9, 11
Psychobiography, 97–100 passim
Psychosexual development, theory of,
    31, 33, 48, 98–100
Putnam, James J., 122

Quantum mechanics, 109

Randall, John Herman, 19
Rank, Otto, 137
Reality principle, 112, 113–14, 115, 117,
    118, 121, 165–66n; science as, 119–20,
    122–23, 124, 126, 129, 142
Religion: victory of science over, 1,
    67–68, 78, 141–45; interpretation of,
    118–19, 126, 141; Freud and, 141–42
Repression, 34, 36–37, 117
Res cogitans, 7, 11, 12, 23, 24, 25, 32,
    52, 54
Res extensa, 7, 24, 27, 52, 54, 65
Ricoeur, Paul, 1, 14, 72
Rieff, Philip, 1

Schopenhauer, Arthur, 110
Sexual selection, 58–59
Sexuality, 15, 47, 49, 56, 57, 58, 59,
    114–16, 131–32; infantile, 60, 98–99,
    100; and neurosis, 60–61; and perver-
    sion, 60–61. *See also* Psychosexual
    development, theory of
Simpson, George Gaylord, 142
Species, 17, 18, 69; concept of, 90,
    93–94
Superego, 130, 131, 139
System theory, 126

Technology, 125, 166–67n
Teleology, 88, 91–94, 96
Temporality, 49–51, 96, 99–100

Unconscious, 8, 36, 38, 39–40, 56,
    70–71, 148, 156–57n, 164n; and con-
    sciousness, 11, 35–38, 114; psychol-
    ogy of, 31, 32, 33, 48, 79, 140–41, 144,
    146–47; and subconscious, 35–36

Weismann, August, 57
Weismannism, 159n
Weltanschauung, scientific, 123–24
Whitehead, Alfred North, 100–01